A LIGHT
UNTO THE
WORLD

A LIGHT UNTO THE WORLD

DAVID B. HAIGHT

DESERET BOOK COMPANY
SALT LAKE CITY, UTAH

Library of Congress Cataloging-in-Publication Data

Haight, David B. (David Bruce), 1906–
    A light unto the world / by David B. Haight.
        p.   cm.
    Includes bibliographical references and index.
    ISBN 1-57345-302-1
    1. Christian life—Mormon authors.   2. Church of Jesus Christ of
Latter-day Saints—Doctrines.   3. Mormon Church—Doctrines.
I. Title.
BX8656.H345   1997
248.4'89332—dc21   97-28688
                                                       CIP

Printed in the United States of America

10 9   8   7   6   5   4   3   2   72082

TO RUBY

I have no greater joy than to hear that
my children walk in truth.

— 3 JOHN 1:4

The David B. and Ruby Olson Haight Family

Ye are the light of the world. A city that is set on an hill cannot be hid. Neither do men light a candle, and put it under a bushel, but on a candlestick; and it giveth light unto all that are in the house. Let your light so shine before men, that they may see your good works, and glorify your Father which is in heaven.

—MATTHEW 5:14-16

CONTENTS

WHATSOEVER IS LIGHT, IS GOOD

THAT WHICH IS
OF GOD IS LIGHT

DOCTRINE AND COVENANTS 50:24

1

A WITNESS
OF DIVINE TRUTHS

S ome time ago, as I was convalescing from a serious operation, I received an unusual card that caused me to ponder upon the majesty of life and immortality. The card featured an original painting by Arta Romney Ballif of the heavens at night with their myriad golden stars. The message, taken from Psalms, read: "Praise ye the Lord: . . . He healeth the broken in heart, and bindeth up their wounds. He telleth the number of the stars; he calleth them all by their names. . . . His understanding is infinite" (Psalm 147:1, 3–5).

As I lay in the hospital bed, I meditated upon all that had happened to me. I studied the contemplative painting by Arta Ballif, a sister of President Marion G. Romney, and the words from the scriptures: "He telleth the number of the stars; he calleth them all by their names." I was then—and continue to be—awed by the goodness and majesty of the Creator, who knows not only the names of the stars but knows your name and my name—each of us as his sons and daughters.

The psalmist David wrote: "When I consider thy heavens, the work of thy fingers, the moon and the stars, which thou hast ordained; what is man, that thou art mindful of him? . . . For thou hast made him a little lower than the angels, and hast crowned him with glory and honour" (Psalm 8:3–5).

To be remembered is a wonderful thing.

The evening of my health crisis, I knew something very serious had happened to me. Events happened so swiftly—the pain striking with such intensity, my dear wife, Ruby, phoning the doctor and our family, and I on my knees leaning over the bathtub for support and some comfort and hoped-for relief from the pain. I was pleading to my Heavenly Father to spare my life a while longer, to give me a little more time to do his work, if it was his will.

While still praying, I began to lose consciousness. The siren of the paramedic truck was the last that I remembered before unconsciousness overtook me, which lasted for the next several days.

The terrible pain and commotion of people ceased. I was now in a calm, peaceful setting; all was serene and quiet. I was conscious of two persons in the distance on a hillside, one standing on a higher level than the other. Detailed features were not discernible. The person on the higher level was pointing to something I could not see.

I heard no voices but was conscious of being in a holy presence and atmosphere. During the hours and days that followed, there was impressed again and again upon my mind the eternal mission and exalted position of the Son of Man. I witness to you that he is Jesus the Christ, the Son of God, Savior to all, Redeemer of all mankind, Bestower of infinite love, mercy, and forgiveness, the Light and Life of the world. I knew this truth before—I had never doubted nor wondered. But now I knew, because of the impressions of the Spirit upon my heart and soul, these divine truths in a most unusual way.

I was shown a panoramic view of his earthly ministry: his baptism, his teaching, his healing the sick and lame, the mock trial, his crucifixion, his resurrection and ascension. There followed scenes of his earthly ministry to my mind in impressive detail, confirming scriptural eyewitness accounts. I was being taught, and the eyes of my understanding were opened by the Holy Spirit of God so as to behold many things.

The first scene was of the Savior and his apostles in the upper chamber on the eve of his betrayal. Following the Passover supper, he gave instruction and prepared the sacrament of the Lord's Supper for his dearest friends as a remembrance of his coming sacrifice. It was so impressively portrayed to me—the overwhelming love of the Savior for each. I witnessed his thoughtful concern for significant details—the washing of the dusty feet of each apostle, his breaking and blessing of the loaf of dark bread and blessing of the wine, then his dreadful disclosure that one would betray him.

He explained Judas's departure and told the others of the events soon to take place.

Then followed the Savior's solemn discourse when he said to the eleven: "These things I have spoken unto you, that in me ye might have peace. In the world ye shall have tribulation: but be of good cheer; I have overcome the world" (John 16:33).

Our Savior prayed to his Father and acknowledged the Father as the source of his authority and power—even to the extending of eternal life to all who are worthy.

Jesus prayed, "And this is life eternal, that they might know thee the only true God, and Jesus Christ, whom thou hast sent." He then reverently added: "I have glorified thee on the earth: I have finished the work which thou gavest me to do. And now, O Father, glorify thou me with thine own self with the glory which I had with thee before the world was" (John 17:3–5).

He pled not only for the disciples called out from the world who had been true to their testimony of him, "but for them also which shall believe on [him] through their word" (John 17:20).

When they had sung a hymn, Jesus and the eleven went out to the Mount of Olives. There in the garden, in some manner beyond our comprehension, the Savior took upon himself the burden of the sins of mankind from Adam to the end of the world. His agony in the garden, Luke tells us, was so intense that "his sweat was as . . . great drops of blood falling . . . to the ground" (Luke 22:44). He suffered an agony and a burden the like of which no human person would be able to bear. In that hour of anguish, our Savior overcame all the power of Satan.

The glorified Lord revealed to Joseph Smith this admonition to all mankind: "Therefore I command you to repent. . . . For behold, I, God, have suffered . . . for all, that they might not suffer if they would repent; . . . which suffering caused myself, even God, the greatest of all, to tremble because of pain, and to bleed at every pore. . . . Wherefore, I command you again to repent, lest I humble you with my almighty power; and that you confess your sins, lest you suffer these punishments" (D&C 19:15–20).

During those days of unconsciousness I was given, by the gift and power of the Holy Ghost, a more perfect knowledge of Jesus' mission. I was also given a more complete understanding of what it means to exercise, in his name, the authority to unlock the mysteries of the kingdom of heaven for the salvation of all who are faithful. My soul was taught over and over again the events of the betrayal, the mock trial, the scourging of the flesh of even one of the Godhead. I witnessed his struggling up the hill in his weakened condition carrying the cross, and his being stretched upon it as it lay on the ground so that the crude spikes could be driven with a mallet into his hands and wrists and feet to secure his body as it hung on the cross for public display.

Crucifixion—the horrible and painful death that he suffered—was chosen from the beginning. By that excruciating death, he descended below all things, as is recorded, so that through his resurrection he would ascend above all things (D&C 88:6).

Jesus Christ died in the literal sense in which we will all die. His body lay in the tomb. The immortal spirit of Jesus, chosen as the Savior of mankind, went to those myriads of spirits who had departed mortal life with varying degrees of righteousness to God's laws. He taught them the "glorious tidings of redemption from the bondage of death, and of possible salvation . . . [which was] part of [our] Savior's foreappointed and unique service to the human family" (James E. Talmage, *Jesus the Christ* [Salt Lake City: Deseret Book, 1977], 671).

I cannot begin to convey to you the deep impact that these scenes have confirmed upon my soul. I sense their eternal meaning and realize that "nothing in the entire plan of salvation compares in any way in importance with that most transcendent of all events, the atoning sacrifice of our Lord. It is the most important single thing that has ever occurred in the entire history of created things; it is the rock foundation upon which the gospel and all other things rest" as has been declared (Bruce R. McConkie, *Mormon Doctrine,* 2d ed. [Salt Lake City: Bookcraft, 1966], 60).

Father Lehi taught his son Jacob and us today:

"Wherefore, redemption cometh in and through the Holy Messiah; for he is full of grace and truth.

"Behold, he offereth himself a sacrifice for sin, to answer the ends of the law, unto all those who have a broken heart and a contrite spirit; and unto none else can the ends of the law be answered.

"Wherefore, how great the importance to make these things known unto the inhabitants of the earth, that they may know that there is no flesh that can dwell in the presence of God, save it be through the merits, and mercy, and grace of the Holy Messiah, who layeth down his life according to the flesh, and taketh it again by the power of the Spirit, that he may bring to pass the resurrection of the dead, being the first that should rise.

"Wherefore, he is the firstfruits unto God, inasmuch as he shall make intercession for all the children of men; and they that believe in him shall be saved" (2 Nephi 2:6–9).

Our most valuable worship experience in the sacrament meeting is the sacred ordinance of the sacrament, for it provides the opportunity to focus our minds and hearts upon the Savior and his sacrifice.

The apostle Paul warned the early Saints against eating this bread and drinking this cup of the Lord unworthily (see 1 Corinthians 11:27–30). Our Savior himself instructed the Nephites: "Whoso eateth and drinketh my flesh and blood unworthily [brings] damnation to his soul" (3 Nephi 18:29).

Worthy partakers of the sacrament are in harmony with the Lord and put themselves under covenant with him to always remember his sacrifice for the sins of the world, to take upon them the name of Christ, and to always remember him and keep his commandments. The Savior covenants that we who do so shall have his Spirit to be with us and that, if faithful to the end, we may inherit eternal life.

Our Lord revealed to Joseph Smith that "there is no gift greater than the gift of salvation," which plan includes the ordinance of the sacrament as a continuous reminder of the Savior's atoning sacrifice. He gave instructions that "it is expedient that the church meet together often to partake of bread and wine in the remembrance of the Lord Jesus" (D&C 6:13; 20:75).

Immortality comes to us all as a free gift by the grace of God alone, without works of righteousness. Eternal life, however, is the reward for obedience to the laws and ordinances of his gospel.

I testify that our Heavenly Father does answer our righteous pleadings. The added knowledge that has come to me has made a great impact upon my life. The gift of the Holy Ghost is a priceless possession and opens the door to our ongoing knowledge of God and eternal joy. Of this I bear witness.

2

EYEWITNESSES OF THE LORD'S MAJESTY

Shortly before the Savior's betrayal and his crucifixion and subsequent resurrection, an event now known as the Transfiguration occurred, which I am sure was meant for the spiritual enlightenment of us as well as for those who were personal witnesses.

The New Testament writers tell us the Savior went up a lofty mountain (Luke says simply "a mountain") to find a secluded spot where he could kneel in prayer and prepare for the events to come. He took with him the three dearest and most enlightened of his apostles.

It must have been early evening when Jesus ascended the mountain with those three chosen witnesses—James and John, the "Sons of Thunder," and Peter, the "Man of Rock." Perhaps Jesus felt not only a sense of the heavenly calm that that solitary opportunity for communion with his Father would bring but also a sense that he would be supported in the coming hour by ministrations not of this earth. He was to be illuminated with a light that needed no aid from the sun or the moon or the stars. He went up to prepare for his coming death. He took his three apostles with him in the belief that they, after having seen his glory—the glory of the Only Begotten of the Father—might be fortified and their faith strengthened to prepare them for the insults and humiliating events that were to follow.

We learn from the scriptures that the Savior, finding a secluded place, knelt and prayed; and as he prayed to his Father, he was elevated far above the doubt and wickedness of the world that had rejected him. As he prayed, he was transfigured. His countenance shone as the sun, and his garments became as white as the snow fields above them. He was enwrapped in an aura of glistening brilliance; his whole presence reflected such a divine radiance that the light of the sun or the white of the snow is the only thing to which the Evangelists can compare that celestial scene. Two figures appeared by his side: Moses and Elias (Elijah). When the prayer was ended and the coming ordeal accepted, the full glory fell upon him from heaven—a testimony of his divine Sonship and power.

Luke's account indicates that the three apostles did not witness the beginning of this marvelous transfiguration. They were heavy with sleep, as they would later be at Gethsemane, but they were suddenly startled into wakefulness (Luke 9:32). Then they saw and heard. In the darkness of the night they saw an intense light and the glorified form of their Lord. Beside him, in that same glory of light, were the two ancient prophets.

As the vision began to fade, Peter, we are told, apparently anxious to delay the departure of the heavenly visitors, expressed the first thought that came to his mind: "Master, it is good for us to be here: and let us make three tabernacles; one for thee, and one for Moses, and one for Elias" (Luke 9:33).

They may have been surprised at the inappropriate proposal made by the eager Peter, who would yet learn the meaning of the night's events. But even as Peter spoke, a bright cloud of brilliant light overshadowed Jesus and his heavenly visitors, Moses and Elijah, and also the three apostles. Then a voice was heard: "This is my beloved Son: hear him" (Luke 9:35).

The three apostles fell prostrate and hid their faces. How long it was before Jesus came to them and touched them is not clear; but when they raised their eyes, it was all over. The bright cloud had vanished; the gleams of light, the shining countenances had passed away; and they were alone with Jesus. Only the light from the stars shone on the mountain slopes.

After such an experience, the apostles may have hesitated to rise; but Jesus, now appearing as they had seen him before he knelt in prayer, touched them and said, "Arise, and be not afraid" (Matthew 17:7). He was their dear friend.

The day was probably dawning as they descended the mountain. Jesus instructed them to tell no one until he had risen from the dead. The vision was for them; they were to ponder it in the depths of their own hearts. They were not even to tell the other apostles. The three disciples kept Christ's instructions but could not understand the full meaning. They could only ask each other, or wonder in silence, what this resurrection from the dead could mean. But they now knew more fully than ever that their Lord was indeed the Christ, the Son of God.

Though it may be difficult for us to understand, Jesus himself must have been strengthened and sustained by Moses and Elijah in preparation for the suffering and agony ahead of him in working out the infinite and eternal atonement of all mankind. In a few days an angel from heaven would again strengthen him when he would sweat great drops of blood in the Garden of Gethsemane.

The three chosen apostles were taught of his coming death and also his resurrection, teachings that would strengthen each of them in the eventful days ahead.

Testifying later, John said, "We beheld his glory, the glory as of the only begotten of the Father" (John 1:14). The apostle Peter, speaking of this personal experience, wrote: "We have not followed cunningly devised fables, when we made known unto you the power and coming of our Lord Jesus Christ, but were eyewitnesses of his majesty. For he received from God the Father honour and glory, when there came such a voice to him from the excellent glory, This is my beloved Son, in whom I am well pleased. And this voice which came from heaven we heard, when we were with him in the holy mount" (2 Peter 1:16–18).

Peter, James, and John. They alone beheld the glory and majesty of the transfigured Jesus and undoubtedly received the keys of the kingdom.

These three were yet to be taken to a spot in Gethsemane where they would behold his suffering as he took upon himself the sins of the world so that he might redeem us from the fall, demonstrate to us through his resurrection that he is the Only Begotten of the Father in the flesh, and show us that he is the Redeemer of the world.

These same three witnesses who were on the mount—Peter, the senior apostle, and James and John—appeared to Joseph Smith and Oliver Cowdery in 1829 to confer upon them the Melchizedek Priesthood and give to them the keys of the kingdom and apostleship. Christ himself, followed by Moses, Elias, and Elijah, appeared to Joseph and Oliver in the Kirtland Temple, giving authority and committing other essential keys of this dispensation. The Prophet wrote of this event:

"In the afternoon, I assisted the other Presidents in distributing the Lord's Supper to the Church, receiving it from the Twelve, whose privilege it was to officiate at the sacred desk this day. After having performed this service to my brethren, I retired to the pulpit, the veils being dropped, and bowed myself, with Oliver Cowdery, in solemn and silent prayer. After rising from prayer, the following vision was opened to both of us" (headnote to D&C 110).

"The veil was taken from our minds, and the eyes of our understanding were opened. We saw the Lord standing upon the breastwork of the pulpit, before us; and under his feet was a paved work of pure gold, in color like amber. . . .

"His voice was as the sound of the rushing of great waters, even the voice of Jehovah, saying: I am the first and the last; I am he who liveth, I am he who was slain; I am your advocate with the Father. . . .

"After this vision closed, the heavens were again opened unto us; and Moses appeared before us, and committed unto us the keys of the gathering of Israel. . . . After this, Elias appeared, and committed the dispensation of the gospel of Abraham, saying that in us and our seed all generations after us should be blessed.

"After this vision had closed, another great and glorious vision burst upon us; for Elijah the prophet, who was taken to heaven without tasting death, stood before us, and said: . . . Therefore, the keys of this dispensation are committed into your hands; and by this ye may know that the great and dreadful day of the Lord is near, even at the doors" (D&C 110:1–4, 11–13, 16).

The divine keys, power, and authority have been committed by heavenly messengers to Joseph Smith in this, the dispensation of the fulness of times. Those keys—the same that were delivered to Peter, James, and John on the mountain—authorize us to carry the true gospel to all nations to declare the power, glory, and majesty of our Lord Jesus Christ and to warn that the day of his coming is near. A prophet of God holds these keys of authority today. We invite people everywhere to inquire further into this divine message we have to offer to all mankind.

3

IN HIM SHALL WE HAVE LIFE

I n the hearts of all persons, of whatever race or station in life, there are inexpressible longings for something they do not now possess. This longing is implanted by a concerned Creator.

A loving Heavenly Father's design is that this longing of the human heart should lead to the one who alone can satisfy it—even Jesus of Nazareth, who was foreordained in the Grand Council before the earth was created. To the brother of Jared, the premortal Jesus said: "Behold, I am he who was prepared from the foundation of the world to redeem my people. Behold, I am Jesus Christ. . . . In me shall all mankind have life, and that eternally, even they who shall believe on my name" (Ether 3:14).

As members of his restored Church, it is imperative that we do our utmost to expand our understanding of his premortal commission, his earthly ministry, his unjust crucifixion, the agony of his suffering, his final sacrifice, and his resurrection. Each of us is profoundly indebted to him, for we were purchased by the shedding of his own precious blood. We are surely obligated to follow his admonition, to believe on his name, and to testify of him and his word.

I am indebted for some of my remarks to eyewitness accounts of Christ's life as recorded in the New Testament; to prophets ancient and modern, especially to the Prophet Joseph Smith for his personal witness that God the Father and his Son live, and for his faithfully following divine instructions in bringing forth the fulness of the everlasting gospel as contained in the Book of Mormon and other latter-day scriptures; to the apostolic writings of Elders James E. Talmage and Bruce R. McConkie; and to others, including theologian and believer Frederic Farrar. Our scriptures teach us gospel truths, and inspired writers add to our understanding.

We have learned that during the last days of his mortal life, Jesus withdrew from all public teaching and spent the Wednesday before Passover in Bethany in seclusion. The next day, Thursday, he instructed Peter and John to go to Jerusalem, where they would find a room prepared so they could meet together. In that room Jesus met with the Twelve, and they sat down to eat.

It was customary that as a person entered a room, he laid aside his sandals at the door and his feet were washed to remove the dust from his travels. A servant usually performed this lowly task, but on this sacred night, "Jesus Himself, in His eternal humility and self-denial, rose from His place at the meal to do [this] menial service" (Frederic W. Farrar, *The Life of Christ* [1874; reprint, Salt Lake City: Bookcraft, 1994], 557).

Jesus said to them: "Ye call me Master and Lord: and ye say well; for so I am. If I then, your Lord and Master, have washed your feet; ye also ought to wash one another's feet" (John 13:13–14).

"He their Lord and Master had washed their feet. It was a kind and gracious task, and such ought to be the nature of all their dealings with each other. He had done it to teach them humility, . . . self-denial, [and] love" (Farrar, *Life of Christ,* 559).

During the course of the meal, Jesus revealed the terrible news that one among them would betray him, and a deep sadness fell over all of them. He then said to Judas, "That [which] thou doest, do quickly" (John 13:27). And Judas left the room to do his awful deed.

Conscious of the impending events, Jesus opened his heart to his chosen eleven, saying: "Now is the Son of man glorified, and God is glorified in him. . . . Little children, yet a little while I am with you. Ye shall seek me: [but] whither I go, ye cannot come. . . . A new commandment I give unto you, That ye love one another; as I have loved you, that ye also love one another. By this shall all men know that ye are my disciples, if ye have love one to another" (John 13:31, 33–35).

While in that upper room, Jesus—initiating the sacrament—took bread, brake it, prayed over it, and passed it to the disciples, saying, "This is my body which is given for you: this do in remembrance of me." And then, passing the cup, he said, "This cup is the new testament in my blood, which is shed for you" (Luke 22:19–20).

The Savior prayed to the Father for the apostles and all believers, saying: "Father, the hour is come; glorify thy Son, that thy Son also may glorify thee: As thou hast given him power over all flesh, that he should give eternal life to as many as thou hast given him. And this is life eternal, that they might know thee the only true God, and Jesus Christ, whom thou hast sent" (John 17:1–3).

The time that remained for him to be with them was short. He told them of the Holy Ghost, whom he would send to comfort and guide them in truth. He taught them many things that night as he tried to prepare them for the things he knew were coming. They then rose from the table, united their voices in a hymn, and left the room together to walk to the Garden of Gethsemane and all that awaited them there.

"The awful hour of His deepest [suffering] had arrived— . . . nothing remained . . . but the torture of physical pain and the poignancy of mental anguish. . . . He . . . calm[ed] His spirit by prayer and solitude to meet that hour in which all that is evil in the Power of [Satan] should wreak its worst upon the Innocent and Holy [One]. And He must face that hour alone. . . . 'My soul,' He said, 'is full of anguish, even unto death.'" It was not the anguish and fear of pain and death but "the burden . . . of the world's sin which lay heavy on His heart" (Farrar, *Life of Christ,* 575–76, 579).

"From the terrible conflict in Gethsemane, Christ emerged a victor. Though in the dark tribulation of that . . . hour He had pleaded that the bitter cup be removed from His lips, . . . the Father's will was never lost sight of" (James E. Talmage, *Jesus the Christ* [Salt Lake City: Deseret Book, 1977], 614).

And then came Judas with his betraying kiss; Christ's surrender to his enemies; the arrest of the Son of God and three sham trials before the priests in the Sanhedrin; the insults and the derision of the multitudes; Christ's appearance before Pontius Pilate, then Herod, then again before Pilate. Then came the final pronouncement of Pilate. After three appeals to the multitude of Jews to spare one of their own fell upon deaf ears, he delivered Jesus to be scourged.

"Scourging was the ordinary preliminary to crucifixion. . . . The . . . sufferer was publicly stripped, was tied . . . to a pillar, and then . . . blows were inflicted with leathern thongs, weighted with jagged . . . bone and lead [or rock]. . . . The victim generally fainted, often died" (Farrar, *Life of Christ*, 624).

When the cross had been prepared, the soldiers placed it upon his shoulders and led him to Golgotha. "But Jesus was enfeebled . . . by [hours] of violent . . . agitation, by an evening of deep . . . emotion, . . . by the mental agony of the garden, by three trials and three sentences of death before the Jews. . . . All these, [added] to the [wounds] of the scourging [and loss of blood], had utterly broken down His physical strength" (Farrar, *Life of Christ*, 634–35). So a bystander was enlisted to carry the heavy cross.

At Calvary, Christ was laid down upon the cross. "His arms were stretched along the cross-beams; and at the center of the open palms, the point of a huge iron nail was placed [and driven through the quivering flesh] into the wood." His feet were also nailed to the cross, which was slowly raised and fixed firmly in the ground. Every movement would be agony to the fresh wounds in his hands and feet. "Dizziness, . . . thirst, . . . sleeplessness, . . . fever, . . . long [hours] of torment. . . . Such was the death to which Christ was doomed" (Farrar, *Life of Christ*, 639, 641).

Jesus was nailed to the cross on that fateful Friday morning, probably between nine and ten o'clock. "At noontide the light of the sun was obscured, and black darkness spread over the whole land. The terrifying gloom continued for a period of three hours. . . . It was a fitting sign of the earth's deep mourning over the impending death of her Creator" (Talmage, *Jesus the Christ*, 660).

At the ninth hour Christ uttered that anguished cry, "My God, my

God, why hast thou forsaken me?" (Matthew 27:46). "In that bitterest hour the dying Christ was alone. [So] that the supreme sacrifice of the Son might be consummated in all its fulness, the Father seems to have withdrawn . . . His immediate Presence, leaving to the Savior of men the glory of complete victory over the forces of sin and death" (Talmage, *Jesus the Christ*, 661).

Later, "realizing that He was no longer forsaken, but that His atoning sacrifice had been accepted by the Father, and that His mission in the flesh had been carried to glorious consummation, He exclaimed in a loud voice of holy triumph: '*It is finished.*' In reverence, resignation, and relief, He addressed the Father saying: '*Father, into thy hands I commend my spirit.*' He bowed His head, and voluntarily gave up His life" (Talmage, *Jesus the Christ*, 661–62).

"At that moment the vail of the Temple was rent in twain from the top to the bottom. An earthquake shook the earth. . . . The multitude, [now] utterly sobered from their furious excitement and frantic rage, . . . returned to Jerusalem" (Farrar, *Life of Christ*, 651–52).

Christ's body was lovingly taken from the cross, placed on fine linen purchased by Joseph of Arimathaea, covered with rich spices, and carried to a nearby garden where a new tomb belonging to Joseph was located.

The next day Pilate gave permission for the tomb to be carefully guarded until the third day, so that the disciples could not steal the body and then tell the people that Jesus had risen from the dead, as had been prophesied. The chief priests and Pharisees made the tomb secure, sealing the stone and leaving a guard on watch (Matthew 27:62–66).

Before daylight the following morning, Mary Magdalene and Mary the mother of James, having prepared fresh spices and ointments, went to the tomb and found that the stone had been rolled away. Looking in and not finding the body, they hurried to find Peter and the apostles and told them what they had found. Peter and John hastened at once to the tomb. John outran his older companion. Stooping down, he gazed in silent wonder into the empty tomb. Peter entered the tomb, where he saw the burial clothes lying where the body of Jesus had once lain. Then John followed him in. Despite their fear, there dawned upon them the hope, which later would become an absolute knowledge, that Christ had indeed risen, but as yet no one had seen him. The two wondering apostles returned to their brethren.

Mary stayed at the tomb and was grieving at the entrance when someone approached. Thinking it was the keeper of the garden, she asked where he had laid her Lord. A voice said to her, "Mary" (John 20:16).

Jesus himself was standing before her, but he did not appear as she had known him; he was now risen and glorified. She then recognized our Lord and must have attempted to embrace him, for he said, "Touch me not; for I am not yet ascended to my Father: but go to my brethren, and say unto them, I ascend unto my Father, and your Father, and to my God, and your God" (John 20:17).

Filled with amazement, she hastened to obey and repeated that glorious message which would give hope through all future ages. To it she added her personal declaration that she had seen the Lord (John 20:18).

Later, women carrying spices for the final preparation of the body for burial looked into the tomb and witnessed angels, who said, "Ye seek Jesus of Nazareth, which was crucified. Why seek ye the living among the dead? He is not here, but is risen" (Mark 16:6; Luke 24:6). The angels told the women to go and notify the disciples, but the men did not believe them (Mark 16:7; Luke 24:9–11).

The Gospel according to Luke relates that on that same day, two of Jesus' followers were on their way to a village called Emmaus, about eight miles from Jerusalem. As they walked and conversed, a stranger joined them and walked along with them. Though this stranger was indeed the resurrected Christ, they did not recognize him.

As the two men approached the village to which they were going, Jesus acted as if he were going further, but they persuaded him to stay, saying, "Abide with us: for it is toward evening, and the day is far spent" (Luke 24:29). So he stayed with them. As he ate the simple meal with them, he took the bread and blessed it; then he broke the bread and gave it to them. As he did this, their eyes were opened, and they recognized the Lord; and then he vanished from their sight.

Stunned, the two men said in amazement to each other, "Did not our hearts burn within us, while he talked with us by the way, and while he opened to us the scriptures?" (Luke 24:32). They hurried back to Jerusalem, where they found ten of the apostles and some other disciples gathered together behind closed doors for fear of the Jews (John 20:19).

They declared, "The Lord is risen indeed, and hath appeared to Simon" (Luke 24:34). Then they explained what had happened on the road and how they had recognized the Lord when he broke the bread.

As the disciples listened, the Lord himself suddenly stood in their midst and said, "Peace be unto you" (Luke 24:36).

They were terrified and supposed that they were seeing a spirit, but he said to them, "Why are ye troubled? and why do thoughts arise in your hearts? Behold my hands and my feet, that it is I myself: handle me, and see; for a spirit hath not flesh and bones, as ye see me have" (Luke 24:38–39). He showed them his hands and his feet. They still could not believe, so he asked, "Have ye here any meat? And they gave him a piece of a broiled fish, and . . . honeycomb." He took the food and ate before them. Then he told them, "These are the words which I spake unto you, while I was yet with you, that all things must be fulfilled, which were written in the law of Moses, and in the prophets, and in the psalms, concerning me" (Luke 24:41–42, 44).

He opened their minds to understand the scriptures, saying, "Thus it is written, and thus it behoved Christ to suffer, and to rise from the dead the third day: and that repentance and remission of sins should be preached in his name among all nations, beginning at Jerusalem." He reminded them, "Ye are witnesses of these things" (Luke 24:46–48).

One of the Twelve, Thomas, was not with them when Jesus came. When the other disciples told him they had seen the Lord, he replied, "Except I shall see in his hands the print of the nails, and put my finger into the print of the nails, and thrust my hand into his side, I will not believe" (John 20:25).

A week later the disciples were again gathered together indoors, and Thomas was with them. The doors were locked, but Jesus came and stood among them and said, "Peace be unto you." Then he said to Thomas, "Reach hither thy finger, and behold my hands; and reach hither thy hand, and thrust it into my side: and be not faithless, but believing" (John 20:26–27).

I have often pictured in my own mind the depth of remorse that must have been burning within Thomas's soul as his doubting heart, now purified, attempted to find a reply to his Lord. Finally he said, "My Lord and my God." And Jesus said to him, "Thomas, because thou hast seen me, thou hast believed: blessed are they that have not seen, and yet have believed" (John 20:28–29).

Perhaps no clearer declaration of fact has ever been made than those facts which tell of the literal resurrection of Christ. The record of appearances to the apostles during the forty days following his resurrection—leaves no cause for doubt. John informs us that "there are also many other things which Jesus did, the which, if they should be written . . . even the world itself could not contain the books that should be written" (John 21:25).

Shortly after his appearance to his disciples in the Eastern Hemisphere, Jesus appeared to the Nephites in the Western Hemisphere. God himself introduced his Son to the multitude: "Behold my Beloved Son, in whom I am well pleased, in whom I have glorified my name—hear ye him" (3 Nephi 11:7).

Elder James E. Talmage has beautifully described the scene: "While gazing upward in reverent expectation, the people beheld a Man, clothed in a white robe, who descended and stood among them. He spake, saying: 'Behold, I am Jesus Christ, whom the prophets testified shall come into the world. And behold, I am the light and the life of the world; and I have drunk out of that bitter cup which the Father hath given me, and have glorified the Father in taking upon me the sins of the world, in the which I have suffered the will of the Father in all things from the beginning.' [3 Nephi 11:10–11.] The multitude [knelt] in adoration for they remembered that their prophets had foretold that the Lord would appear among them after His resurrection and ascension. As He directed, the people arose, and one by one came to Him, and did see and feel the prints of the nails in His hands and feet and the spear-wound in His side. . . . With one accord they cried: 'Hosanna! blessed be the name of the Most

High God' [3 Nephi 11:17]. Then, falling at the feet of Jesus, they worshipped Him" (Talmage, *Jesus the Christ*, 673–74).

When Joseph Smith was visited by the Father and the resurrected Christ in 1820, the latter was introduced by the Father, thus ushering in the marvelous events of the restoration of the gospel of Jesus Christ.

Our resurrected Lord was seen in a vision by Joseph Smith and Sidney Rigdon in 1832. Joseph recorded: "The Lord touched the eyes of our understandings. . . . And we beheld the glory of the Son, on the right hand of the Father, and received of his fulness; and saw the holy angels, and them who are sanctified before his throne, worshiping God, and the Lamb, who worship him forever and ever. And now, after the many testimonies which have been given of him, this is the testimony . . . which we give of him: That he lives! For we saw him, even on the right hand of God; and we heard the voice bearing record that he is the Only Begotten of the Father—that by him, and through him, and of him, the worlds are and were created, and the inhabitants thereof are begotten sons and daughters unto God" (D&C 76:19–24).

These fragmentary events that I have briefly portrayed bear record and witness that resurrection and eternal life come to us because of what Christ our Lord did for each of us. He declared, "I am the resurrection, and the life: he that believeth in me, though he were dead, yet shall he live: and whosoever liveth and believeth in me shall never die" (John 11:25–26). To this declaration of truth I bear my solemn witness.

4

THE MISSION
OF JOSEPH SMITH

Since my early youth, I have always believed and carried in my mind a vivid picture of the youthful Joseph Smith finding a secluded spot, kneeling in the quiet grove, and in faith asking the desire of his heart. He must have felt assured that the Lord would hear and somehow answer him. There appeared to him two glorious personages, a description of whom, he said, was beyond his ability to express.

As the years have passed, with my many experiences with people, places, study, prayer, and personal events of an intimate, spiritual nature, I have been blessed with an ever-deepening faith and knowledge and witness of this heavenly restoration of the Lord's work. The events of the Restoration related by Joseph Smith are true. We who labor in this cause can develop in our bosoms an uplifting, sanctifying, and glorifying feeling of its truth. The Holy Ghost will reveal and seal upon our hearts this knowledge.

Our understanding of and belief and faith in the vision of the Father and the Son to Joseph, which ushered in this final dispensation with its great and precious truths, are not only essential but are also the basis for the authority to proclaim to the people of the world that Jesus Christ is the Only Begotten Son in the flesh of our Eternal Father and is the

Redeemer of the world. We declare that salvation comes only through him and that Joseph Smith is the instrument, or revealer, of that knowledge. We declare that Joseph was given the keys of salvation for all mankind and that The Church of Jesus Christ of Latter-day Saints is the Lord's church and kingdom on earth, the only true and living church having the power to teach and administer saving ordinances on the earth.

We testify and teach that God did reveal himself unto Joseph Smith, the witness of this final dispensation. God has made known unto us that Jesus Christ is in the express image of the Father, and we now know something of the form, features, and even character of that mighty intelligence whose wisdom, creation, and power control the affairs of the universe.

In the Prophet Joseph Smith's own words, the brightness of his vision was above anything he had ever known. He looked up and beheld two glorious personages. One of them, pointing to the other, said, "*This is My Beloved Son*. Hear Him!" (Joseph Smith–History 1:17). Surely it must have seemed inconceivable to young Joseph that he was looking upon God our Father and his Son, and that the Lord had come to visit and instruct him.

The Son, being bidden by the Father, spoke to the kneeling boy. Joseph was told that all the churches were wrong. They had corrupted the doctrine, broken the ordinances, and lost the authority of the priesthood of God. He was told that the leaders of the man-made churches were displeasing to the Lord, collecting money that should be given freely; and that the time of the restoration of all truth and authority had come, including the organization of the Church of Jesus Christ. Then, to his infinite astonishment, Joseph learned that he—humble, unlearned, young—was to be the instrument through whom the Almighty would reestablish his work in these, the latter days. Such was the beginning of the restoration of the Church of Jesus Christ.

Some three years later, Joseph Smith had another heavenly visitation, this time from an angel sent from the presence of God. The angel, who informed Joseph that his name was Moroni, revealed the resting place of a set of gold plates upon which certain ancient inhabitants of America had recorded the history of their peoples. In course of time, these records were to be translated by Joseph, through the gift and power of God. The manuscript was published early in 1830 as the Book of Mormon. It is the most remarkable book in the world from a doctrinal, historical, or philosophic point of view. Its integrity has been assailed with senseless fury for over a century and a half, yet its position and influence today are more impregnable than ever.

The Book of Mormon did not come forth as a curiosity. It was written with a definite and very important purpose, a purpose to be felt by every reader. From the title page, we read that it was written "to the convincing of the Jew and Gentile that Jesus is the Christ, the Eternal God, manifesting himself unto all nations." The message it contains is a witness for Christ and teaches the love of God for all mankind. Its purpose is to bring people to accept Jesus as the Christ. The most important part of the book tells of the actual visit of Christ to ancient America and records the teachings and instructions he gave in clarity and great power to the people. The Book of Mormon substantiates the Bible in its teachings of the Savior; it speaks of Christ more than any other subject and teaches that he is the Redeemer and Atoner of mankind, the central figure in God's plan of salvation.

I have marveled at God's wisdom in bringing forth this ancient record in the manner in which it was accomplished, for it becomes the powerful witness of the divine mission of Joseph Smith.

On Sunday, 28 November 1841, the Prophet wrote: "I spent the day in council with the Twelve Apostles at the house of President Young, conversing with them upon a variety of subjects. . . . I told the brethren that the Book of Mormon was the most correct of any book on earth, and the keystone of our religion, and a man would get nearer to God by abiding by its precepts, than by any other book" (*History of The Church of Jesus Christ of Latter-day Saints,* ed. B. H. Roberts, 2d ed. rev., 7 vols. [Salt Lake City: The Church of Jesus Christ of Latter-day Saints, 1932–51], 4:461).

Joseph Smith was foreordained to be the duly appointed leader of this, the greatest and final of all dispensations. After the angel Moroni's visit, other heavenly messengers conferred upon him holy priesthood authority, divine keys, power, and numerous revelations from God.

Not only was the Church organized under inspiration and divine direction but through Joseph Smith, the necessary body of doctrine for guidance of the Church was also revealed. Faith and light were again available to dispel the darkness that had been upon the earth. Joseph Smith, after seeking and being taught by the Author of Truth, learned that:

1. God is in form like a man.

2. God has a voice—he speaks.

3. God is considerate and kind.

4. God answers prayers.

5. God's Son, Jesus Christ, is obedient to the Father and is the mediator between God and man.

6. "The Father has a body of flesh and bones as tangible as man's; the Son also; but the Holy Ghost has not a body of flesh and bones, but is a personage of Spirit" (D&C 130:22).

Joseph also learned about a new concept of man—his past, present, and future state—with an understanding of the continuity of intelligence and eternal progression. And though Hebrew scriptures refer to temples and baptism for the dead, Joseph Smith was the first person in this dispensation to have revealed to him the purpose of temples and salvation for the dead and the eternal marriage covenant and sealing of man and woman as the foundation for exaltation.

Under the inspiration of Almighty God, the Church began to flourish. The Lord had promised that a great and "marvelous work is about to come forth" (D&C 4:1), and it was spreading rapidly and in a miraculous way. The missionary spirit was touching hearts. The Book of Mormon was being read. Tens, then hundreds, and then thousands joined the Church. Politicians began worrying over this new phenomenon. Enemies were organizing, and by 1844 the Prophet's life was in serious danger.

In his last public address to a large congregation in Nauvoo, Joseph said: "I do not regard my own life. I am ready to be offered a sacrifice for this people; for what can our enemies do? Only kill the body, and their power is then at an end. Stand firm, my friends; never flinch. Do not seek to save your lives, for he that is afraid to die for truth will lose eternal life. . . . God has tried you. You are a good people; therefore I love you with all my heart. Greater love hath no man than that he should lay down his life for his friends. You have stood by me in the hour of trouble, and I am willing to sacrifice my life for your preservation" (*History of the Church,* 6:500).

This statement is all the more remarkable because the Prophet was still in the morning of life—only thirty-eight years old—and great as he had already become, the zenith of his mental and spiritual powers had not yet been reached. Life, with all its possibilities of future achievements, was precious to him. Yet he was willing to give it up, willing to forgo all the honors that might be his, the greatness that would come to him if he lived.

Parley P. Pratt declared: "Had he been spared a martyr's fate till mature manhood and age, he was certainly endued with powers and ability to have revolutionized the world in many respects, and to have transmitted to posterity a name associated with more brilliant and glorious acts than has yet fallen to the lot of mortals" (*Autobiography of Parley P. Pratt* [Salt Lake City: Deseret Book, 1985], 32).

As Joseph Smith left Nauvoo for Carthage that 24th day of June, he would have looked for the last time on the city and the magnificent temple that he loved. He knew that he would never look upon it again. To his companions who were accompanying him, he gave these prophetic words: "I am going like a lamb to the slaughter, but I am calm as a summer's morning. I have a conscience void of offense toward God and toward all men. . . . It shall be said of me 'He was murdered in cold blood!'" (*History of the Church,* 6:555).

Why did he not turn back? There was time to escape. He was not yet in the hands of his enemies. Friends were at his side who would die for him, if necessary. Some suggested that he flee across the Mississippi, where he would be safe. But he continued on to Carthage.

Joseph must have recalled some of the dangers through which he had passed, such as the winter night when a mob broke into his home, tore him from the bedside of his wife and sick children, and dragged him over the frozen ground for a hundred yards or more, kicking and beating him until he fainted. When consciousness returned, they stripped him of his clothing and covered his naked body with a coat of tar and feathers, forcing open his mouth to fill it with the same substance. Then they left him on the frozen ground to die of cold and exposure.

He might have recalled the time in Missouri when he and some of his brethren had been betrayed into the hands of their enemies by a traitor in the Church. The leader of the mob convened a court-martial, and Joseph and his associates were placed on trial for their lives. They were not even permitted to be present at the trial. They were convicted and all sentenced to be shot at eight o'clock the next morning on the public square in Far West. At the appointed hour they were duly led forth to be murdered, but a dispute among the mob leaders saved them for the time being. The sentence was not revoked, however. Without even being permitted to bid farewell to their families, they were taken from place to place and exhibited to jeering crowds, while the Saints were told that they would never see their leaders again.

While in prison, Joseph cheered his fellow prisoners by announcing that none of them would suffer death. "Be of good cheer, brethren," he said; "the word of the Lord came to me last night that our lives should be given us, . . . not one of our lives shall be taken" (*History of the Church*, 3:200n).

As Joseph contemplated those dreary months of imprisonment, he must have recalled that one night when, confined in a dungeon, he rebuked the guards. He and his brethren were trying to get a little sleep, but they were kept awake by the awful blasphemies and obscene jests of their jailers, who told of the dreadful deeds of robbery and murder that they had committed among the Mormons. This was no idle boast, for these awful crimes had actually been committed. Suddenly Joseph rose to his feet and, in a voice that seemed to shake the very building, cried out: "*Silence,* ye fiends of the infernal pit! In the name of Jesus Christ I rebuke you, and command you to be still; I will not live another minute and hear such language. Cease such talk, or you or I die *this instant!*" (*History of the Church,* 3:208n).

The effect must have been electrifying. Some of his jailers begged his pardon; others slunk into the dark corners of the room as if to hide their shame. The power of Jesus Christ, whose name Joseph had invoked in his rebuke, was upon him. His hands and feet were in chains, but these the guards did not see. They saw only the righteous anger in his shining face, and felt the divine power in his voice as he rebuked them.

But if Joseph's voice was as terrible as a roaring lion in his rebuke of the wicked, it was as soothing as a mother's voice in comfort to the righteous. In that same name and by the same authority with which he silenced the blasphemies of the guards, he blessed little children, baptized repentant sinners, conferred the Holy Ghost, healed the sick, and spoke words of comfort and consolation to thousands.

At midnight, when the wagon journey from Nauvoo ended, Joseph and his brethren entered Carthage, and his fate was sealed. His enemies had awaited their coming with great anxiety. The governor, who was present, persuaded the mob to disperse that night by promising them that they should have full satisfaction. The next day, after a hearing, Joseph was released on bail, but he was subsequently rearrested on a trumped-up charge of treason. Bail was now refused, and he was placed in Carthage Jail.

The last night of Joseph's life on earth, he bore a powerful testimony to the guards and others assembled at the door of the jail, telling them of the divinity of the Book of Mormon and declaring that the gospel had been restored and the kingdom of God had been established on the earth. It was for this reason that he was incarcerated in prison, not because he had violated any law of God or man.

Late at night Joseph and his companions tried to get some rest. At first Joseph and his brother Hyrum occupied the only bed in the jail cell, but a gunshot fired during the night and a disturbance led Joseph's friends to insist that he take a place between two of them on the floor. They would protect him with their own bodies. Joseph asked Stephen Markham to use his arm for a pillow while they conversed; then he turned to Dan Jones, on the other side, and whispered, "Are you afraid to die?" And this staunch friend answered, "Has that time come, think you? Engaged in such a cause, I do not think death would have many terrors."

Joseph replied, "You will yet see Wales, and fulfill the mission appointed you before you die" (*History of the Church,* 6:600–601).

The next morning, the fateful 27th of June, 1844, three of the brethren left the prison, and only four remained—Joseph and Hyrum Smith, John Taylor, and Willard Richards. They spent the day in writing letters to their wives, conversing on principles of the gospel, and singing. Between three and four o'clock in the afternoon, the Prophet asked Elder Taylor to sing "A Poor Wayfaring Man of Grief." This comforting song breathes in every line the very spirit and message of Christ. Only a person who loved his Savior and his fellowmen could have desired to hear these words at such a time.

When Elder Taylor had finished the song, Joseph asked him to sing it again, which he did. This time his voice was more sad and tender than at first, and when he concluded, all voices were hushed, but four hearts beat quicker as they listened to the fateful words:

> My friendship's utmost zeal to try,
> He asked, if I for him would die;
> The flesh was weak; my blood ran chill,
> But the free spirit cried, "I will!"

While this spirit of love and service for men, expressed in song and prayer, filled the hearts of all within the jail, the mob was gathering. Within little more than an hour, Joseph and Hyrum had been killed and John Taylor wounded. Only Willard Richards was unharmed.

When the news of the awful crime reached Nauvoo, the citizens were overcome with grief and horror. Probably such universal sorrow had never been known in an American city before. Their prophet and their patriarch were dead. What else mattered?

When the wagon carrying the bodies from Carthage was still a long way off, the entire population of Nauvoo went out to meet it. No greater tribute was ever paid to mortal man than was paid that day to Joseph and Hyrum Smith. Such universal love from those who loved them best could never have been won by selfish and designing men. Only love begets love. Once when Joseph was asked how he got so many followers and retained them, he replied, "It is because I possess the principle of love. All I can offer the world is a good heart and a good hand" (*Teachings of the Prophet Joseph Smith,* sel. Joseph Fielding Smith [Salt Lake City: Deseret Book, 1938], 313).

John Taylor wrote of him: "Joseph Smith, the Prophet and Seer of the Lord, has done more, save Jesus only, for the salvation of men in this world, than any other man that ever lived in it. In the short space of twenty years, he has brought forth the Book of Mormon, which he translated by the gift and power of God, and has been the means of publishing it on two continents; has sent the fulness of the everlasting gospel, which it contained, to the four quarters of the earth; has brought forth the revelations and commandments which compose this book of Doctrine and Covenants, and many other wise documents and instructions for the benefit of the children of men; gathered many thousands of Latter-day Saints, founded a great city, and left a fame and name that cannot be slain. He lived great, and he died great in the eyes of God and his people; and like most of the Lord's anointed in ancient times, has sealed his mission and his works with his own blood" (D&C 135:3).

I testify that in the year 1820 God the Eternal Father and his Son, Jesus Christ, appeared to Joseph Smith, who was foreordained to be the instrument of the Restoration, which is The Church of Jesus Christ of Latter-day Saints, and that this Church, by divine direction, is preparing for Christ's second coming.

5

WE THANK THEE,
O GOD, FOR A PROPHET

Friends who are not members of our church have asked me, "How do you justify your declarations of your church being the true church? Is your claim of authority more valid than that of other churches?" My answer is always, "Yes. We possess the same divine priesthood authority that was held anciently."

At the time the Savior and his twelve apostles were laboring along the coast of Caesarea Philippi, the Savior asked them, "Whom do men say that I the Son of man am?" They answered: "Some say that thou art John the Baptist: some, Elias; and others, Jeremias, or one of the prophets." He asked them, "But whom say ye that I am?" Peter answered, "Thou art the Christ, the Son of the living God."

Jesus responded: "Blessed art thou, Simon Bar-jona: for flesh and blood hath not revealed it unto thee, but my Father which is in heaven. And I say also unto thee, that thou art Peter, and upon this rock I will build my church; and the gates of hell shall not prevail against it. And I will give unto thee the keys of the kingdom of heaven: and whatsoever thou shalt bind on earth shall be bound in heaven: and whatsoever thou shalt loose on earth shall be loosed in heaven" (Matthew 16:13–19).

The Lord's statement teaches that it was upon the power of revelation that the Church should be built. The keys of the kingdom were to be given to Peter; and later, as he associated with the other members of the Twelve, he exercised this power as he presided over them.

The Bible describes a number of occasions when the Savior took only Peter, James, and John with him and evidently gave them additional instructions. He took these three apostles up on the Mount, where they were witnesses of his glorified transfiguration, and where they received the promised keys of the priesthood. This heavenly event included the appearance of Moses and Elias. The apostles also heard the voice of the Father bearing witness that Jesus is his beloved Son, and the command that they were to listen and obey.

In September 1830, Joseph Smith and Oliver Cowdery were ordained to the Melchizedek Priesthood by Peter, James, and John, and the keys were restored to Joseph Smith.

By revelation the Lord told the Prophet, "I will drink of the fruit of the vine with you on the earth, . . . and also with Peter, James and John, whom I have sent unto you, by whom I have ordained you and confirmed you to be apostles, and especial witnesses of my name, and bear the keys of your ministry . . . ; unto whom I have committed the keys of my kingdom, and a dispensation of the gospel for the last times; and for the fulness of times, in the which I will gather together in one all things, both which are in heaven, and which are on earth" (D&C 27:5, 12–14).

When the Lord by revelation called Frederick G. Williams and Sidney Rigdon to serve as counselors to Joseph Smith, he said, "Hearken to the calling wherewith you are called, even to be a high priest in my church, and a counselor unto my servant Joseph Smith, Jun.; whom I have given the keys of the kingdom, which belong always unto the Presidency of the High Priesthood" (D&C 81:1–2).

In the Kirtland Temple on 3 April 1836, the heavenly beings who had appeared to the Savior and his three apostles on the Mount appeared and conferred additional priesthood authority and keys upon Joseph Smith and Oliver Cowdery, for the gathering of Israel, the saving work for the dead, and the building up of the Church preparatory to the coming of Christ to rule and reign on the earth forever.

These keys of the kingdom that were held by Peter, James, and John, who served as the First Presidency in the dispensation of the meridian of time, and that were conferred upon Joseph Smith, are held by the president and prophet of the Church today. He holds this supreme authority. He holds the right of revelation and of decision for the priesthood and for the Church.

William Fowler, a British convert of 1849, was so moved by the very thought of a prophet of God living among the people that he wrote these stirring words: "We thank thee, O God, for a prophet to guide us in these latter days."

Through our prophet we receive the tried and proven principles of the gospel. In a revelation given through Joseph Smith a few months after the Church was organized, the Lord gave careful instructions and counsel to the new leaders to "ask of God, who giveth liberally; and that which the Spirit testifies unto you even so I would that ye should do in all holiness of heart. . . . Seek ye earnestly the best gifts, always remembering for what they are given; . . . they are given for the benefit of those who love me and keep all my commandments."

The Lord goes on to explain: "For all have not every gift given unto them; . . . [but] to every man is given a gift by the Spirit of God. . . . To some it is given by the Holy Ghost to know that Jesus Christ is the Son of God. . . . To others it is given to believe on their words" (D&C 46:7–9, 11, 13–14).

The work we have been assigned to do has been placed by the Almighty in the hands of a prophet. He is the mouthpiece of the Lord for today. The Lord, speaking to the Church in this dispensation and referring to the early leaders, said: "They shall speak as they are moved upon by the Holy Ghost. And whatsoever they shall speak when moved upon by the Holy Ghost shall be scripture, shall be the will of the Lord, shall be the mind of the Lord, shall be the word of the Lord, shall be the voice of the Lord, and the power of God unto salvation" (D&C 68:3–4).

How are we to know and receive direction for ourselves and our families? By personal revelation in answer to our humble prayers and by being in tune with the counsel of our prophet. The Lord has always communicated to his people through his prophets. The Lord's spokesmen are not self-appointed but are called of God. When Joseph Smith was called to be "a seer, a translator, a prophet, an apostle of Jesus Christ," the Lord declared in a revelation: "Wherefore, . . . thou shalt give heed unto all his words and commandments which he shall give unto you as he receiveth them, walking in all holiness before me; for his word ye shall receive, as if from mine own mouth, in all patience and faith. For by doing these things the gates of hell shall not prevail against you; yea, and the Lord God will disperse the powers of darkness from before you, and cause the heavens to shake for your good, and his name's glory" (D&C 21:1, 4–6).

Our prophet holds all the keys for the Church to accomplish its divine mission: to preach the gospel to every nation and people, to organize stakes of Zion throughout the world, for the gathering of Israel, to build holy temples for performing of sacred ordinances for the living and for the dead, and for the worldwide gathering of the Lord's people in preparation for the second coming of the Savior. There is only one person at the head of the Church on the earth at one time. No man can take it unto himself. He must be called of God as was Aaron (see Hebrews 5:4).

On 6 April 1830, the day the Church was organized, the Lord gave this commandment to the Church: "For his [the Church president's] word ye shall receive, as if from mine own mouth, in all patience and faith. . . . For thus saith the Lord God: Him have I inspired to move the cause of Zion in mighty power for good" (D&C 21:5–7).

Our fifth Article of Faith declares: "We believe that a man must be called of God, by prophecy, and by the laying on of hands by those who are in authority, to preach the Gospel and administer in the ordinances thereof."

The revealed process by which a man becomes the president of the Church begins when he is called, ordained, and set apart to become a member of the Quorum of the Twelve Apostles—a call that is inspired of the Lord. That calling and ordination place the newly called apostle in a priesthood quorum with eleven other men who hold the apostleship. Each apostle is ordained under the direction of the president of the Church, who holds the keys of all of the kingdom of God. He gives to each new apostle the priesthood authority necessary for him to hold every position in the Church.

We declare that the authority to administer in the name of God is operative in The Church of Jesus Christ of Latter-day Saints today. We further testify that this power, or commission, was conferred on the first officers of the Church by ordination under the hands of those who held the same power in earlier dispensations. Joseph Smith received the keys of the apostleship from Peter, James, and John, who held the authority of the apostleship in the New Testament times. This authority has come down from the Prophet Joseph Smith to our current president.

During the days of Joseph Smith, there were some who were pretenders to apostolic authority. One such was an elder who was sent by Joseph Smith to preach the gospel. It was not long until this elder proclaimed himself a high priest and said he had been ordained by an angel from heaven. He deceived some Church members. He was called back to Ohio by the Prophet Joseph Smith and questioned about his claims. He soon confessed that he had lied, and he begged forgiveness. Orson Hyde, one of the Twelve Apostles, recorded the principle that the Prophet then taught all those who were assembled in the School of the Prophets:

"No true angel from God will ever come to ordain any man, because they have once been sent to establish the priesthood by ordaining me thereunto; . . . the priesthood being once established on earth, with power to ordain others, no heavenly messenger will ever come to interfere with that power by ordaining any more. . . . You may therefore know, from this time forward, that if any man comes to you professing to be ordained by an angel, he is either a liar or has been imposed upon in consequence of transgression by an angel of the devil, for this priesthood shall never be taken away from this church" ("Although Dead, Yet He Speaketh," *Millennial Star,* 20 Nov. 1846, 139).

These instructions should be a warning and testimony to any pretender who claims apostolic authority on the basis that he has been visited by angels. It should also be a warning to anyone who may be so deceived as to follow these false shepherds.

I have been impressed with all of the prophets since the time of the Prophet Joseph Smith—he who by revelation received the message, the visit from God the Father and his Son. I know that in order to usher in this work, that visitation took place, giving the Prophet Joseph Smith the vision and the determination and the ability to withstand all that he did to help bring about the Restoration. Heavenly messengers and revelations came to the Prophet Joseph Smith to help usher in this great work, which we declare to all the world and which I know to be true. I know that the prophets who have followed since the time of the Prophet Joseph Smith were all called of God.

6

THIS WORK IS TRUE

A short time ago I stood in a family circle while the husband of one of our granddaughters blessed their new little son, Mark. As he blessed Mark, he prayed that he would someday go on a mission and, when he returned, find a sweet, young companion and be sealed in the temple. As he pronounced these blessings upon little Mark, I had the desire that he might know what I know and feel what I feel about some of the spiritual blessings that have entered into my life. I desired that his life would also be filled with spiritual experiences similar to one I had when I was called to be an assistant to the Quorum of the Twelve Apostles.

I remember the details well. I was called to the First Presidency's office to meet with President Joseph Fielding Smith. His name would be presented the next day for sustaining as the new president and prophet of the Church. Harold B. Lee was to be sustained as the first counselor and N. Eldon Tanner as the second counselor in the First Presidency. They spent a few moments with me, extending the call, and then reminded me that the next morning my name would be read in the conference.

After that call was extended to me, I walked down the granite steps of the Church Administration Building. I felt amazement and wonder. *How could this happen? How could this come to me?* As I walked around the block, I thought and wondered about the changes that would come into my life now. *How would I ever measure up to the responsibility that would now rest upon me? How could I go out in the world and represent this great and glorious organization?* I was so overcome with my feelings as I walked around the block that I didn't want to meet anyone I knew. I just wanted to find my wife, Ruby, and tell her what had happened. I went up to the ninth floor of the Hotel Utah, where Ruby was visiting with some family members. I remember knocking on the door and opening it just a couple of inches so I could motion for her to come out. Of course, she wondered what was happening and came out into the hall.

I took her by the hand, and as we walked along the hallway, all I could do was squeeze her hand. I was so overcome with what had happened that I had trouble even getting the words out to tell her about it. Finally she stopped me and said, "Well, say something." Then I looked at her, put my hands on her shoulders, and told her what had happened. She started to cry. The two of us stood there with our arms around each other. Our lives had been changed. The next day, my name was read to be sustained, and I was asked to come up and take one of those red chairs. I did so in all amazement. And then the Tabernacle Choir sang "O Divine Redeemer." I thought my heart would break in the pleading of those words: "Remember not, remember not, O Lord, my sins."

I would hope someday that our great-grandson Mark and others of our posterity would have similar spiritual experiences and that they would feel the spiritual power and influence of this gospel. I hope that Mark and others will have the opportunities such as I had when I was in the temple when President Spencer W. Kimball received the revelation regarding the priesthood. I was the junior member of the Quorum of the Twelve. I was there. I was there, with the outpouring of the Spirit in that room so strong that none of us could speak afterwards. We just left quietly to go back to the office. No one could say anything because of the powerful outpouring of the heavenly spiritual experience.

Just a few hours after the announcement was made to the press, I was assigned to attend a stake conference in Detroit, Michigan. When my plane landed in Chicago, I noticed an edition of the *Chicago Tribune* on the newsstand. The headline in the paper read "Mormons Give Blacks Priesthood." And the subheading said "President Kimball Claims to Have

Received a Revelation." I bought a copy of the newspaper and stared at one word in that subheading—*claims*. It stood out to me just as if it had been in red neon. As I walked along the hallway to make my plane connection, I thought, *Here I am now in Chicago walking through this busy airport, yet I was a witness to this revelation. I was there. I witnessed it. I felt that heavenly influence. I was part of it.* Little did the editor of that newspaper realize the truth of that revelation when he wrote, " . . . Claims to Have Received a Revelation." Little did he—or the printer, or the man who put the ink on the press, or the one who delivered the newspaper— little did any of them know that it was truly a revelation from God. Little did they know what I knew because I was a witness to it.

President Spencer W. Kimball was a great influence in my life. How he taught us! In his wonderful manner, he taught from the scriptures and discussed principles and policy and doctrine in a way that would help lift our hearts and souls. He told a story of a young soldier who had gone into the army. He had written a letter home to his parents saying that he had been at the shooting range learning how to handle a rifle and that he had been taught how to handle a hand grenade. This young man wrote, "In learning how to handle a hand grenade, we were throwing duds, ones that weren't real." Then he said, "When we were throwing duds, I was able to get thirty-five feet away, but today they gave us the real thing and I got eighty feet away." President Kimball could touch our lives in a way that helped us see and understand things to be done.

On 1 October 1994, we sustained as God's prophet on earth another kind, sensitive servant of God—Howard William Hunter. He was a humble, faithful, scholarly, and gentle soul, one who experienced deep sorrow and suffered serious infirmities and even a threat upon his life, but, with his Scottish ancestral determination, he never gave in or gave up.

President Hunter understood compassion, thankfulness, graciousness, charity, and gratitude toward individuals and toward mankind, and he had the saintly bearing of a prophet of God. He was in my estimation, truly Christlike.

In calling him to the apostleship in October 1959, President David O. McKay said to him, "The Lord has spoken. You are called to be one of his special witnesses, and tomorrow you will be sustained as a member of the Council of the Twelve" (quoted in Eleanor Knowles, *Howard W. Hunter* [Salt Lake City: Deseret Book, 1994], 144).

A prophet is one who knows by personal revelation from the Holy Ghost that Jesus Christ is the Son of God, for "the testimony of Jesus is the spirit of prophecy," as the Prophet Joseph taught us (Revelation 19:10; *Teachings of the Prophet Joseph Smith,* sel. Joseph Fielding Smith [Salt Lake City: Deseret Book, 1938], 119). Thus every prophet bears record of Jesus Christ. The sermons, writings, and teachings of President Hunter attest that he was indeed a prophet and a special witness of our Lord and Savior. He declared:

"As one called and ordained to bear witness of the name of Jesus Christ to all the world, I testify . . . that he lives. He has a glorified, immortal body of flesh and bones. He is the Only Begotten Son of the Father in the flesh. He is the Savior, the Light and Life of the world. Following his crucifixion and death, he appeared as a resurrected being to Mary, to Peter, to Paul, and to many others. He showed himself to the Nephites. He has shown himself to Joseph Smith, the boy prophet, and to many others in our dispensation. This is his church; he leads it today" (*Ensign,* May 1988, 17).

The Prophet Joseph Smith taught, "Every man who has a calling to minister to the inhabitants of the world was ordained to that very purpose in the Grand Council of heaven before this world was." He continued, "I suppose I was ordained to this very office in that Grand Council" (*Teachings of the Prophet Joseph Smith,* 365). God's hand directs this work. He prepares his servants. He knows their hearts. He knows the end from the beginning and raises up those servants who will carry out his designs.

An early apostle, Elder Orson Hyde, said: "It is invariably the case, that when an individual is ordained and appointed to lead the people, he has passed through tribulations and trials, and has proven himself before God, and before His people, that he is worthy of the [position] which he holds. . . . Some one that understands the Spirit and counsel of the Almighty . . . is the [one] that will lead the Church" (in *Journal of*

Discourses, 26 vols. [London: Latter-day Saints' Book Depot, 1854–86], 1:123).

No man better understands the Church, nor is better known to the members of it, than our living prophet, President Gordon B. Hinckley.

I testify that he has been carefully prepared for this divine calling from before the foundations of the earth in heavenly councils.

He was born into a family of faith, people who were devoted to the precious truths of salvation as contained in the holy scriptures and the revelations received by the Prophet Joseph Smith. His parents set lofty examples and taught him how to work and to finish a task, which inspired him to attain a good education and a desire to serve mankind.

He accepted the challenges of missionary work and gained the blessings of sharing the gospel with others when called as a missionary to England.

New talents were developed as he assisted his mission president in London in developing Church publicity for the media and for the members of the Church and for the world. That interest has continued throughout his years and continues on to the present day.

His responsibilities in the Church missionary program added new methods and opportunities to proclaim gospel principles, and he was instrumental in expanding missionary work, particularly throughout the vast, teeming Orient, in a most remarkable way.

He has participated in the dedication and rededication of more temples than any other presiding officer in the Church. That is not only indicative of his love for temple work, but it reflects the necessity for us to be actively involved in the work of redeeming our deceased ancestors.

His marriage on 29 April 1937 to his sweetheart, Marjorie Pay, added spiritual strength and increased desire to advance our Lord's work. She has been a most inspiring companion these many years.

President Hinckley is not only a man for all seasons—but for all the world!

In April 1996, following the Sunday sessions of general conference, we went home to watch a television program. We were concerned for President Hinckley, who was to appear on a nationwide television program. We knew of the importance of this appearance and what it would mean to us. We knew of the work and the hours of prayer and meditation and study that our prophet and leader had done in being prepared for this exposure, which would reach some 35 million people.

After that program was over, my heart was beating fast, and I felt it would burst. I was filled with joy and thanksgiving to the Lord for the way our prophet and our leader had handled the interrogation by one who had a reputation of attempting to ask questions that might be difficult to handle. What a joy it was for us to witness how our prophet and our leader had been blessed and magnified! As I watched his face on the television, I realized that a vast number of people were seeing what a prophet of God looked like: a kind, good, and handsome man, clean and intelligent. You could see the outstanding character, the personality of our prophet and leader. And then when the interrogator asked him, "Do you really believe that story that heavenly beings appeared to that young boy in that grove of trees? Do you really believe that to be true?" our prophet instantly said, "Of course I do. Isn't it great?"

Those words have been ringing through my ears ever since that happened: "Of course I do. Isn't it great?" He made that pronouncement with such confidence and with that wonderful personality he has, declaring it to all of the world. Since that time, missionary activity in the United States in the areas where people who heard that program reside has picked up, and member activity has picked up, too. More people have become interested in the Church because they have seen a living prophet in the flesh stand before that immense audience and declare to the world, "Of course I do. Isn't it great?" We hope and pray that the missionaries throughout the world have that same feeling and that same understanding and that same determination—to want to so declare this message of hope and salvation and eternal life to all the world.

I thank the Lord every day for the health and determination I have to make the best use of every hour I have upon the earth to help in the spreading of this work. I know it is true.

7

WHY DO WE BUILD TEMPLES?

Temples are the most sacred places of worship on earth where sacred ordinances are performed—ordinances that pertain to salvation and exaltation in the kingdom of God. Each one is literally a house of the Lord—a place where he and his Spirit may dwell, where he may come or send others to confer priesthood blessings and to give revelation to his people.

Temples built especially to the Lord have been erected in all ages. Moses built a tabernacle in the wilderness for the children of Israel. Solomon built a magnificent temple in Jerusalem. The Nephites built sacred temples. Joseph Smith built houses of the Lord in Kirtland and Nauvoo, and succeeding prophets have built temples throughout the world. These have all been initiated and built under the direction and revelation of God.

Without revelation, temples can neither be built nor properly used. They are one of the evidences of the divinity of our Lord's true gospel. In our day, the Lord has said: "How shall your washings be acceptable unto me, except ye perform them in a house which you have built to my name? . . . that . . . ordinances might be revealed which had been hid from . . . the world" (D&C 124:37–38).

Latter-day Saints should be eternally grateful for the revealed knowledge given anciently but reaffirmed in even greater plainness in our dispensation, knowledge that was known by our Lord's apostle Peter when he prophesied that before the second coming of Christ there would be a "restitution of all things" as spoken of by God (Acts 3:21; D&C 121:26–32). One of these restored doctrines, premortality, or pre-earth existence, should give us a greater appreciation for ourselves and the work assigned us, for each one of us existed as a spirit entity before we were born on this earth.

Most of us have wondered about what occurred in the premortal world and how it relates to our existence here. We should be acquainted with the truth that knowledge of the premortal life was restored in order that we might fulfill our responsibilities as children of God.

The Lord has revealed that a grand council was held in that pre-earth world where we exercised our free agency regarding the plans presented. The major proposition in the accepted plan of salvation provided for an earth life where each person could work out his eternal salvation.

Elder John A. Widtsoe provides important insight to an earth-life responsibility made in that premortal world. He highlights a contractual agreement we made concerning the eternal welfare of all of the sons and daughters of the Eternal Father:

"In our preexistent state, in the day of the great council, we made a[n] . . . agreement with the Almighty. The Lord proposed a plan. . . . We accepted it. Since the plan is intended for all men, we became parties to the salvation of every person under that plan. We agreed, right then and there, to be not only saviors for ourselves but . . . saviors for the whole human family. We went into a partnership with the Lord. The working out of the plan became then not merely the Father's work, and the Savior's work, but also our work. The least of us, the humblest, is in partnership with the Almighty in achieving the purpose of the eternal plan of salvation."

Elder Widtsoe continues:

"That places us in a very responsible attitude towards the human race. By that doctrine, with the Lord at the head, we become saviors on Mount

Zion, all committed to the great plan of offering salvation to the untold numbers of spirits. To do this is the Lord's self-imposed duty, this great labor his highest glory. Likewise, it is man's duty, self-imposed, his pleasure and joy, his labor, and ultimately his glory" ("The Worth of Souls," *Utah Genealogical and Historical Magazine*, Oct. 1934, 189).

Latter-day Saints are a chosen people, so appointed in the premortal world, to be in partnership with the Lord for the salvation of the living and the dead. The First Presidency has announced that one of the major responsibilities of the Church, and therefore of its members, is to redeem the dead.

We learn by revelation from the Prophet Joseph Smith that "these are principles in relation to the dead and the living that cannot be lightly passed over, as pertaining to our salvation. For their salvation is necessary and essential to our salvation. . . . For we without them cannot be made perfect; neither can they without us be made perfect" (D&C 128:15, 18; Hebrews 11:39–40).

It would be difficult to find stronger language on a requirement to receive exaltation in the celestial kingdom.

Joseph Smith and Oliver Cowdery received the Melchizedek Priesthood under the hands of Peter, James, and John; however, it was necessary for the prophet Elijah to restore special keys "in order that all the ordinances may be attended to in righteousness" (Joseph Smith, *History of The Church of Jesus Christ of Latter-day Saints*, ed. B. H. Roberts, 2d ed. rev., 7 vols. [Salt Lake City: The Church of Jesus Christ of Latter-day Saints, 1932–51], 4:211). Thus, the sealing powers and ordinances necessary for the dead as well as the living were to be restored. This was accomplished by Elijah's visit to Joseph and Oliver on 3 April 1836 in the Kirtland Temple.

Elijah's mission was to "turn the heart of the fathers to the children, and the heart of the children to their fathers" (Malachi 4:6). The turning of the hearts of the fathers in the spirit world to the children on earth provides for the gathering of ancestral data of their deceased fathers in order that ordinances might be performed in the temples of the Lord. Thus, the living having their hearts turned to their fathers is in accordance with the premortal agreement we made before the earth was formed.

Elijah's visit to the Kirtland Temple is attested by several truths.

First, no one else has claimed that the prophecy regarding Elijah's coming in the last days has been fulfilled.

Second, the testimony of Joseph Smith and Oliver Cowdery stands unassailable—they could not turn the hearts of the children to the fathers except by the power sent by God.

Third, neither did they have the power to persuade millions of people to turn their attention to their deceased fathers. Remarkable indeed is the fact that organized efforts to gather genealogical information began after Elijah came in 1836. In America, the New England Historical and Genealogical Society was organized in 1844, and the New York Genealogical and Biographical Society in 1869, for the purpose of gathering genealogy. What is known as the "Spirit of Elijah" has influenced nonmembers as well as members of the Church in this vital activity. The microfilming of thousands of records is continuing on a large scale throughout the world.

The Jewish people have looked forward to the return to the earth of Elijah as promised by Malachi. Each year in the spring the Paschal feast is observed in many Jewish homes, at which time a door is opened so that Elijah might come in and sit at the feast.

"It was . . . on the third day of April, 1836," said President Joseph Fielding Smith, "that the [Jewish people], in their homes at the Paschal feast, opened their doors for Elijah to enter. [However,] on that very day Elijah did enter—not in the home of the Jews to partake of the Passover with them, but he appeared in the House of the Lord . . . in Kirtland, and there bestowed his keys" (in Conference Report, Apr. 1936, 75).

The Prophet Joseph said the main object of the gathering of the Jews, or of the people of God in any age of the world, was "to build unto the Lord a house whereby He could reveal unto His people the ordinances of His house and the glories of His kingdom, and teach the people the way of salvation" (*Teachings of the Prophet Joseph Smith,* sel. Joseph Fielding Smith [Salt Lake City: Deseret Book, 1938], 307–8).

Bible prophecies indicate that in the last dispensation of the gospel, there would be a restoration of all of the principles and practices of former dispensations, which includes temple building and the performing of ordinances therein (Isaiah 2:2–3; Micah 4:1–2; Acts 3:19–21; Ephesians 1:9–10).

A latter-day apostle, Elder Hyrum M. Smith, wrote: "The history of Temples teaches us that the people of God have been strong, or weak, in proportion to the faithfulness with which they have attended to their sanctuaries" (Hyrum M. Smith and Janne M. Sjodahl, *Doctrine and Covenants Commentary* [Salt Lake City: Deseret Book, 1951], 612).

We would do well to follow the example of our late beloved prophet, President Ezra Taft Benson. He and his sweet companion, Flora, set aside time each Friday to regularly attend the house of the Lord. They would join with me in declaring that members of the Church who absent themselves from temple attendance, where it is possible for them to attend, are denying themselves rich blessings. In latter-day revelation we learn: "Whatever principle of intelligence we attain unto in this life, it will rise with us in the resurrection. And if a person gains more knowledge and intelligence in this life through his diligence and obedience than another, he will have so much the advantage in the world to come. There is a law, irrevocably decreed in heaven before the foundations of this world, upon which all blessings are predicated—And when we obtain any blessing from God, it is by obedience to that law upon which it is predicated" (D&C 130:18–21).

With these scriptures in mind, I exhort all members to a renewed commitment in strengthening their faith and progression to exaltation in the celestial kingdom—

First, by fulfilling our responsibility to our dead. The Prophet Joseph said, "The greatest responsibility in this world that God has laid upon us, is to seek after our dead" (*Times and Seasons,* 5:616). I am indebted to my kindred dead who made it possible for me to live in this dispensation and to have the privilege of being a member of the "only true and living church upon the face of the whole earth" (D&C 1:30).

Our opportunities are twofold: to do genealogical research and to perform temple work. There may be a time when we may not be able to do the research required, but this should not deter us from receiving the blessings of temple attendance. With an increasing number of functioning temples located in many parts of the world, the privilege of participating in temple activity is becoming more and more available. Should you or I neglect either of these responsibilities?

Second, by being "endowed with power from on high" (D&C 38:32). The environment in the temple is intended to provide the worthy member of the Church with the power of enlightenment, of testimony, and of understanding. The temple endowment gives knowledge that, when acted upon, provides strength and conviction of truth.

Third, by finding a place of refuge and peace (D&C 124:36). The moment we step into the house of the Lord, the atmosphere changes from the worldly to the heavenly, where respite from the normal activities of life is found, and where peace of mind and spirit is received. It is a refuge from the ills of life and a protection from the temptations that are contrary to our spiritual well-being. We are told that "he who doeth the works of righteousness shall receive his reward, even peace in this world, and eternal life in the world to come" (D&C 59:23).

Fourth, by receiving revelation. John A. Widtsoe wrote: "I believe that the busy person on the farm, in the shop, in the office, or in the household, who has his worries and troubles, can solve his problems better and more quickly in the house of the Lord than anywhere else. If he will . . . [do] the temple work for himself and for his dead, he will confer a mighty blessing upon those who have gone before, and . . . a blessing will come to him, for at the most unexpected moments, in or out of the temple will come to him, as a revelation, the solution of the problems that vex his life. That is the gift that comes to those who enter the temple properly" ("Temple Worship," *Utah Genealogical and Historical Magazine,* Apr. 1921, 63–64).

Revelation also comes in receiving greater understanding of the endowment as one seeks to comprehend its meaning.

Fifth, by giving genealogical and temple service. The Prophet Joseph Smith wrote: "Those saints who neglect it in behalf of their deceased relatives, do it at the peril of their own salvation" (*History of the Church,* 4:426).

Sixth, by becoming saviors on Mount Zion. The Prophet Joseph wrote: "But how are they to become saviors on Mount Zion? By building their temples, . . . and receiving all the ordinances, . . . ordinations and sealing powers upon their [own] heads, [and] in behalf of all their progenitors who are dead, and redeem them that they may come forth in the first resurrection and be exalted to thrones of glory with them; and herein is the chain that binds the hearts of the fathers to the children, and the children to the fathers, which fulfills the mission of Elijah" (*History of the Church,* 8:184).

And seventh, by qualifying to see and understand God in the house of the Lord. At Kirtland, the Lord revealed to the Prophet Joseph: "And inasmuch as my people build a house unto me in the name of the Lord, and do not suffer any unclean thing to come into it, that it be not defiled, my glory shall rest upon it; . . . and my presence shall be there, for I will come into it, and all the pure in heart that shall come into it shall see God" (D&C 97:15–16).

It is true that some have actually seen the Savior, but when one consults the dictionary, he learns that there are many other meanings of the word *see,* such as coming to know him, discerning him, recognizing him and his work, perceiving his importance, and coming to understand him.

Such heavenly enlightenment and blessings are available to each of us.

8

COME TO THE
HOUSE OF THE LORD

In the first recorded revelation of this, the last dispensation, our Lord instructed Joseph Smith in what we regard as perhaps the greatest work of this dispensation: to seal the living to their families and progenitors (D&C 2).

Inscribed on brass plaques in the entry of the Alberta Temple are these significant words written by Orson F. Whitney, an apostle of eighty years ago:

> Hearts must be pure to come within these walls,
> Where spreads a feast unknown to festive halls.
> Freely partake, for freely God hath given,
> And taste the holy joys that tell of heaven.
> Here learn of Him who triumphed o'er the grave.
> And unto men the keys, the kingdom gave;
> Joined here by powers that past and present bind
> The living and the dead perfection find.

These tender words remind those who enter the temple of significant truths about their service in the temple: that all who enter may do so feeling the love of our Heavenly Father.

"Hearts must be pure." With this phrase Elder Whitney teaches the importance of effective preparation to attend the temple. We who would attend the temple must be living in a manner that helps us be worthy to enter and fully partake of the feast of which he spoke.

We examine our worthiness to enter the temple in our annual temple recommend interviews with priesthood leaders. Our signature, with theirs, on our temple recommend testifies of our worthiness to enter the temple. How important it is to be completely honest with our bishop. To be less than completely honest with him about our worthiness creates a breach of integrity that compounds the seriousness of concealed sins.

When we present our recommend to the attendant at the temple, we reaffirm our worthiness to enter the temple. If an unresolved problem exists since we received the recommend, it would be well to obey our Lord's teaching expressed in his Sermon on the Mount:

"Therefore if thou bring thy gift to the altar, and there rememberest that thy brother hath ought against thee; Leave there thy gift before the altar, and go thy way; first be reconciled to thy brother, and then come and offer thy gift" (Matthew 5:23–24).

Remember that the gifts we bring to his house are not the sacrifices our ancestors of old brought to their temples, but the pure hearts of which Brother Whitney speaks. We apply the Lord's direction by ensuring that our hearts are pure by examining our lives before we approach his house. Where there is an unresolved sin, we should take the necessary penitent action to clear it.

We should also examine our relationships with our brothers, our sisters, our wife or husband, our children, our parents, or anyone else who might have "ought against us." We should repair and strengthen any damaged relationship, then come to the temple.

The truly humble and obedient take this preparation a step further. They clear their hearts of any feelings that may be out of harmony with the sacred environment and sacred experiences they will encounter in the temple. They will be mindful that feelings of anger, hostility, fear, frustration, haste, or any preoccupation with matters outside the temple will interfere with their ability to fully partake of the feast available within the temple, which is a feast of the Spirit. Those kinds of feelings are left outside the temple when we enter.

A temple is a place in which those whom the Lord has chosen are endowed with power from on high—a power that enables us to use our gifts and capabilities with greater intelligence and increased effectiveness in order to bring to pass our Heavenly Father's purposes in our own lives and in the lives of those we love.

As he dedicated the cornerstone of the Salt Lake Temple on 6 April 1853, President Brigham Young made this observation about the endowment: "Your *endowment* is, to receive all those ordinances in the House of the Lord, which are necessary for you, after you have departed this life, to enable you to walk back to the presence of the Father, passing the angels who stand as sentinels, . . . and gain your eternal exaltation in spite of earth and hell" (in *Journal of Discourses,* 26 vols. [London: Latter-day Saints' Book Depot, 1854–86], 2:31).

We receive the blessings of which President Young spoke when we are endowed. Our understanding of the significance of the endowment expands as we regularly participate in the holy ordinances in behalf of those deceased.

Some participate more fully in the feast of which Orson F. Whitney spoke than do others. Those who receive the most understand the teaching methods the Lord uses in the temple. They bring to the temple hearts and minds prepared to participate in the Lord's way of learning.

Others receive less and may be somewhat disappointed in their temple experience; perhaps they do not understand how the Lord teaches us in his house. Elder John A. Widtsoe said: "We live in a world of symbols. No man or woman can come out of the temple endowed as he should be, unless he has seen, beyond the symbol, the mighty realities for which the symbols stand" ("Temple Worship," *Utah Genealogical and Historical Magazine,* Apr. 1921, 62).

If you may have been somewhat confused, unclear, or concerned about your temple experience, I hope you will return again and again. When you return, come with an open, seeking, contrite heart, and allow the Spirit to teach you by revelation what the symbols can mean to you and the eternal realities which they represent. Elder Widtsoe thoughtfully provided some counsel about how you might do this. He spoke of the Prophet's first vision as a model of how revelation, in the temple and elsewhere, is received.

"How do men receive revelations?" he asked. "How did the Prophet Joseph Smith obtain his first revelation, his first vision? He desired something. In [a grove of trees], away from human confusion, he summoned all the strength of his nature; there he fought the demon of evil, and, at length, because of the strength of his desire and the great effort that he made, the Father and the Son descended out of the heavens and spoke eternal truth to him" (Widtsoe, "Temple Worship," 63).

Elder Widtsoe observed that the strength of Joseph's desire and the great effort he exerted were what enabled him to receive his vision of the Father and the Son. Desire and effort are likewise required if we would receive revelation to understand the ordinances of the endowment. He wrote: "Revelation . . . is not imposed upon a person; it must be drawn to us by faith, seeking and working. . . . To the man or woman who goes through the temple, with open eyes, heeding the symbols and the covenants, and making a steady, continuous effort to understand the full meaning, God speaks his word, and revelations come. . . . The endowment which was given by revelation can best be understood by revelation; and to those who seek most vigorously, with pure hearts, will the revelation be greatest" ("Temple Worship," 63). Revelation comes in response to our desire and seeking; then we feast on the "holy joys that tell of heaven."

President Ezra Taft Benson gave us a promise about this. He said: "Now by virtue of the sacred priesthood in me vested, . . . I promise you that, with increased attendance in the temples of our God, you shall receive increased personal revelation to bless your life as you bless those who have died" (in Conference Report, Apr. 1987, 108).

Come to the temples worthily and regularly. Not only do we bless those who are deceased, but we may freely partake of the promised personal revelation that may bless our lives with power, knowledge, light, beauty, and truth from on high, which will guide us and our posterity to eternal life. What person would not want these blessings? At the dedication of the Kirtland Temple, the Prophet Joseph Smith prayed: "We ask thee, Holy Father, that thy servants may go forth from this house armed with thy power, and that thy name may be upon them, and thy glory be round about them, and thine angels have charge over them" (D&C 109:22).

When we return from the temple, we should share with our children and loved ones at home our feelings about what we experienced. We should not speak of the sacred ordinances but of the love and power manifest by them.

Let our children see us behave—toward them and our eternal companion—in kindlier, more loving ways. Consistently positive expressions about what we experience in the temple will create in our children a desire to receive those same blessings and provide them with strong motivation to resist the temptations that could disqualify them from temple blessings.

Through the exercise of the sealing power of the holy priesthood, generations are bound together in patriarchal chains from the newborn baby "as far back as the Lord shall reveal" (Brigham Young, in *Journal of Discourses,* 3:372).

When sweethearts kneel at the temple altar and are joined by the power of the holy priesthood for time and all eternity, an eternal family is organized and is created. It is to exist throughout all eternity. It may become eternal in its attributes by the constant fidelity of a husband and wife to each other and by their faithfulness to their covenants with their Heavenly Father.

If you are sealed to a spouse, whether living or departed, recall for a moment your memories of that day of days when you knelt together at the altar and were sealed as husband and wife for time and all eternity. Do you remember any of the words of the ceremony? Do you recall sacred feelings, a glimpse of eternal promises? Can you feel again the power that created a relationship which will transcend death? Can you recall the feeling of love of our Heavenly Father for you and your companion, which was manifest on that occasion?

If time and the realities of everyday life have eroded your recollections of what you felt and received when you were sealed, you should return to the temple and participate again as proxies for the departed in that same sealing ordinance. Take advantage of that opportunity. Do it together as husband and wife. In this manner you may deepen your understanding of the covenants you made and renew the promises you received on that day when you were sealed as eternal companions.

For some people, these words may reopen wounds they wish closed and buried. There may be a bitter tinge to the memories they invoke because that which once seemed so glorious and promising little resembles the reality they now experience. Their eternal marriage may have been destroyed by infidelity or apostasy, or perhaps it is being eroded by indifference, neglect, or inattention to covenants. Perhaps such a person has been a faithful spouse but is now involuntarily a lonely, struggling, single parent.

To that individual I would say: May your heart be lifted by my testimony, that your faithfulness to your endowment and sealing covenants assures you a fulness of the blessings promised. The infidelity, sin, or indifference of a spouse need not adversely affect *your* faithfulness to *your* covenants. I testify to you that the promised blessings are yours through your faithfulness to your covenants. I testify that no matter how long and difficult the road, you can, with the support of loving leaders and the constant love of our Savior, arrive at your eternal destination.

And to those who may not now qualify for a temple recommend, I would say: Work with your priesthood leaders and change your life in order to worthily enter the temple. Then attend regularly. You will come to know our Lord there. As your relationship with him grows and deepens, you will grow increasingly confident in his love, in his compassion for your difficulties, in his power to bear you up and bring you back into his presence. As you avail yourself of that divine assistance, you will come to know that there can be no challenge, no difficulty, no obstacle in your life which you and he together cannot overcome. To that I testify!

Each of the ordinances of the Lord's house bears witness "of Him who triumphed o'er the grave"—of the reality of his atonement and his resurrection. We are taught of immortality and eternal life, which are realities for us through his atonement. We are blessed by covenants and ordinances to prepare us to eventually reenter his divine presence. I pray that we will each take full advantage of every opportunity to regularly come to our Lord's temple and there freely partake of the feast and blessings he provides.

9

OUR LABOR FOR OUR ANCESTORS

During the public showing of the San Diego California Temple in the spring of 1993, more than seven hundred thousand people took advantage of that opportunity to see the temple. The first two days of the open house were set aside for state and local civic leaders, clergy of other faiths, business and education leaders, as well as for the media and the press. Several hundred accepted the invitation. It was my privilege, along with others, to welcome and speak to these guests and answer their questions.

Early in the morning on the first day, ignoring the rain, these invited guests stood in line to enter a house of the Lord. They quietly and reverently walked through the temple gazing in amazement at the architectural beauty and appointments fitting a house of the Lord. They came to see for themselves what they had heard and read about.

Rabbi Wayne Dosick wrote in the *San Diego Jewish Times:* "The Temple is built . . . of earthly materials to construct a place that inspires heavenly awe. This Mormon Temple uses sweeping architecture to create a space that invokes the celestial heavens that is awesome." He continued, "We thank them for reminding us how holy a place a mere building can be" ("Open House Update," *San Diego Jewish Times,* 20 Mar. 1993).

Many moving accounts came to our attention as a result of this open house; countless hearts were touched. More than eight thousand individuals with special needs came in wheelchairs, each bringing relatives or friends to assist them. One young boy paused at the entrance to the temple to carefully clean and polish the wheelchair his father was in before entering the sacred interior of the temple. A devoted father lifted his frail fifteen-year-old daughter in his arms as he carried her from her wheelchair into the bride's dressing room. She looked around and said, "Oh, this is so beautiful." With a smile on her lips and with tears in her eyes, she gently laid her head on her father's shoulder and said, "This is where I want to come to be married someday." This young girl had come to the temple from the hospital, where she has spent most of the past five years—her wish to see the temple fulfilled.

Those who attended the open house not only were touched by its beauty, but notes and comments indicated that many felt a deep reverence and profound emotional impact.

For more than one hundred years that same feeling has entered the hearts of vast numbers of visitors to Temple Square as they have seen and felt the majesty and unsurpassed beauty of the Salt Lake Temple. A century after its dedication, it proudly stands as a regal monument of the faith, industry, and vision of the Saints of God who built it.

But even more majestic than the temple itself is the vision of the purpose of temples that guided the builders. That purpose is to redeem all mankind who are obedient to the laws and commandments of God.

In seeking after our dead ancestors, we may have visions of tedious poring over musty books and microfilms and years of searching, unless we possess the vision of this great latter-day work and understand how to proceed. The Church Family History Department has microfilmed vital records for about two billion individuals. All that we have to do for a given ancestor is hope his or her records exist—and then find them.

Yes, it isn't always easy. But as you pursue your search, keep these three principles in mind:

First, the Lord never asks the impossible. Often the difficult, but never the impossible.

Some may feel that they have conscientiously sought the Spirit in the task of finding ancestral information without success and therefore attribute their lack of success to insufficient faith. If you have felt this way, I suggest patience. Give the Lord time. Have faith that in his due time, all of the information you need will become available. But in the meantime, ask the Lord to direct your attention to other ancestors whose information is more accessible.

There is also available to you another valuable source of help. Knowledgeable family history consultants are now available in your ward and stake to assist you in your searching for your ancestors.

Second, begin where you are. Take one step at a time. You know key information about the lives of your parents. Record their information and then move backward, a generation at a time, watching for unbaptized, unendowed, and unsealed ancestors.

Third, don't try to do everything at once. King Benjamin taught: "And see that all these things are done in wisdom and order; for it is not requisite that a man should run faster than he has strength" (Mosiah 4:27).

Prayerfully determine what you should do for your ancestors. Many factors affect this—what other family members might have done already, your own abilities and interests, the time you have available. But it is important that you do something.

Regular temple attendance is one of the simplest ways you can bless those who are waiting in the spirit world. If you live near a temple, partake of the opportunity to go often and regularly. If you live some distance from a temple, plan excursions so that you, too, might be uplifted and edified through this most satisfying and much-needed labor of love.

Eighty-three-year-old Luella Boyd, a widow, would leave her home in Basin, Wyoming, at five o'clock in the morning, drive seven hours to the temple in Idaho Falls, arriving about noon, and then participate in four endowment sessions. The next morning she would be at the temple when it opened and attend eight more sessions, going without lunch. On the third day she would start at 5:00 A.M. and complete four endowments by noon—then drive home to Basin, Wyoming, arriving at 8:00 P.M. Sixteen sessions—six hundred miles—three days—eighty-three years old! One year she did this eleven times, missing only one month because of bad weather. The most exceptional part of this story is that she also served in her eighties as a family history missionary in Salt Lake City. What a marvelous spirit and dedication!

Now, after you have accomplished the temple work for your immediate ancestors, identify the difficult-to-find ancestors, serve in Family Record Extraction, or create a computer version of your family records to share with family members and others through the Church's Ancestral File™. All of these activities help provide the sacred ordinances of the temple for your ancestors. If you will do this, you will know the indescribable joy of being a savior on Mount Zion to a waiting ancestor whom you have helped.

The Lord has poured out his Spirit upon his children—which is manifest in new technology, simplified procedures, and expanding resources, which enable us to accelerate our progress in the redemption of the dead.

When we have conscientiously done all we can to locate records of our ancestors, the Lord will direct our attention to obscure records in unlikely places where ancestral information has been preserved.

A dedicated family history missionary could not read the microfilm information for one woman. He could not decipher it. He knelt at his work area to ask the Lord for help, but he could not read the microfilm. He knelt again and petitioned the Lord, but still he could not read it. The third time he knelt down and suggested to the Lord that he felt that this woman was waiting for her work to be done, and if he couldn't read the microfilm, how could this take place? As he got up and looked at the microfilm again, it was perfectly clear.

I believe that when we diligently seek after our ancestors—in faith—needed information will come to us, even when no mortal records of their lives are available.

Our labor for our ancestors is part of the divine plan of our Heavenly Father. It is a momentous assignment given to his Church, which we *will* complete because he has ordained it. This work is a powerful witness of the divine mission of Joseph Smith, through whom it was revealed.

Elder John A. Widtsoe made this remarkable statement: "When the history of human thought shall be written from the point of view of temple worship, it may well be found that temples and the work done in them have been the dominating influence in shaping human thought from the beginning of the race. Even today," he continued, "political controversies are as nothing in determining the temper of a people, as compared with religious sentiments and convictions, especially as practiced in the temples of the people" ("Temple Worship," *Utah Genealogical and Historical Magazine,* Apr. 1921, 52).

The salvation of our Heavenly Father's children from Adam and Eve to the present generation is the most important work in time and eternity. Our joy—or our disappointment—in the eternities may hinge on our willing participation in this great latter-day work.

President Spencer W. Kimball said, "The more clearly we see eternity, the more obvious it becomes that the Lord's work . . . is one vast and grand work with striking similarities on each side of the veil" ("The Things of Eternity—Stand We in Jeopardy?" *Ensign,* Jan. 1977, 3).

God bless us to love our ancestors and to be worthy of temple participation.

LIGHT IS COME INTO THE WORLD

JOHN 3:19

10

MISSIONARY WORK: OUR RESPONSIBILITY

Some time ago, joy and nostalgia dominated our conversation as Sister Haight and I drove to the airport to see our eleventh grandchild leave for his mission. During our brief visit—with warm greetings and emotional embraces—we recalled some of the historical accounts of how the message of the restoration of the gospel had influenced our family, of how our missionary grandson's great-great-grandfather, Joseph Toronto, heard and believed the message of the gospel from missionaries in Boston in 1843.

Joseph Toronto assisted with the building of the Nauvoo Temple. Brigham Young had made a strong appeal on Sunday, 6 July 1845, for the Saints to remember to pray for the temple and to pay their tithing. The Saints were anxious that the temple be finished sufficiently so that ordinance work might begin before the exodus westward. More workers and tithing were desperately needed. Joseph Toronto, a new convert, visited Brigham Young after the meeting and declared that "he wanted to give himself and all he had to the kingdom of God." He handed President Young twenty-six hundred dollars in gold coins. President Young blessed the Italian convert, proclaiming that "he should stand at the head of his race and that neither he nor his family should ever want for bread." Later, in 1849, Joseph was called to accompany the new apostle Lorenzo Snow to his native Italy to open that land for the preaching of the gospel ("Italian Pioneer," *Church News,* 20 June 1981, 16; *Joseph Toronto: Italian Pioneer and Patriarch,* Toronto Family Organization, 1983, 10).

My wife and I also spoke of Hector C. Haight, another ancestor, called from his home in Farmington, Utah, to preside over the Scandinavian Mission in 1856 with little or no ability to speak Danish, Swedish, or Norwegian. But trusting in the Lord and with the assistance of the Scandinavian Saints, he accomplished his assignment. He reported in 1858 that "2,610 souls had been baptized . . . and [that] 990 members had emigrated to Zion" (Andrew Jenson, *History of the Scandinavian Mission* [Salt Lake City: Deseret News Press, 1927], 128).

These ancestors, along with many others, gave inspiration and set the precedent of love for the gospel and its divine truth and for missionary service, which our children and grandchildren inherit but must personally acquire for themselves.

Our hearts were filled that morning as we again witnessed the miracle that had already begun and that we knew would continue—not only for the next two years but for the rest of his life—the transformation of a fine young man into a powerful proclaimer and believer of our Lord Jesus Christ. Our gratitude for and trust in the missionary program of the Church, in all of its spiritual dimensions, and for its continuing influence on our family were deepened and strengthened.

While watching family expressions of love and joy and tears at the airport, I thought of the hundreds of young men and women and couples who, week after week, leave our missionary training centers around the world to embark on the grandest experience of their lives: going forth to serve our Heavenly Father with all of their heart, might, mind, and strength. That is indeed one of the great miracles of our time.

An article in the *Church News* told of Aaron Thatcher, a young man with a love for baseball. Many baseball scouts had observed Aaron's unique talents, but he told them repeatedly that he would not sign a professional contract until after he had fulfilled his obligations to the Lord by serving a two-year mission.

"How could a young man turn down such an offer?" people asked. But he did! His desire to serve the Lord was greater than his desire for instant fame. Aaron explained, "I'm going on this mission not because . . . my dad went. I'm going because I have a testimony of the gospel and the prophets have told us that every worthy and healthy young man should serve a full-time mission. I want to with all of my heart" (in Quig Nielsen, "Baseball 'On Hold' While He Serves Mission," *Church News*, 4 Sept. 1993, 5).

The Lord is opening the way and making it possible to expand his work throughout the world, and what a blessing it is for all of us—each in his own way—to take part.

In recent years, the number of missionaries serving throughout the world has grown to more than fifty thousand. The number of missions has increased to more than three hundred. Nearly one and one-half million new converts joined the Church in a recent five-year period. And our missionaries or representatives have been teaching in more than forty additional countries where they were not serving five years before.

Who but the prophets of God could have foreseen the miracle of the rapid expansion of the work of the Lord? Truly, as the Lord foretold in Section 88 of the Doctrine and Covenants, he is hastening his work in its time (D&C 88:73).

I am inspired as I continue to understand more and more the depth and significance of the vision and inspiration the Prophet Joseph Smith received from heavenly messengers as he carefully laid in place the foundation stones of the restored Church. After what he had experienced and knew, the Prophet Joseph Smith could boldly write in March 1842:

"Our missionaries are going forth to different nations, . . . the Standard of Truth has been erected; . . . the truth of God will go forth boldly, nobly, and independent, till it has penetrated every continent, visited every clime, swept every country, and sounded in every ear, till the purposes of God shall be accomplished, and the Great Jehovah shall say the work is done" (*History of The Church of Jesus Christ of Latter-day Saints*, ed. B. H. Roberts, 2d ed. rev., 7 vols. [Salt Lake City: The Church of Jesus Christ of Latter-day Saints, 1932–51], 4:540).

There is a spirit moving upon our people to want to live their lives in harmony with truth, that they may someday respond to an opportunity to serve. This is the same spirit and heavenly influence that directed John Taylor, Wilford Woodruff, and others to take leave of the Saints from the city of Far West, Missouri, early on the morning of 26 April 1839, as they departed for their missions to Great Britain (D&C 118:4–5). On that occasion each prayed in turn at the temple site and bore testimony. Then, after a song, they took leave, directed by revelation, filled with the blessings of heaven and the confirming influence of the Holy Ghost. These early apostles departed for their missions having been spiritually fed and blessed in a manner that would sustain them and their families throughout their many hardships and inspire their powerful testimonies of the truthfulness of the message of the restored Church upon the earth.

What a privilege and a blessing to be a small part of this great work! With that heritage, however, comes a great responsibility. The Lord needs messengers to match his message. He needs those who are able to wield the mighty and eternal influence that he has placed in their hands. In Section 88, where the Lord speaks of hastening his work, he gives to the laborers of his kingdom a commandment to "prepare yourselves, and sanctify yourselves; yea, purify your hearts, and cleanse your hands and your feet before me, that I may make you clean" (D&C 88:74).

The calling to serve the Lord places a tremendous, ennobling responsibility upon each of us. President Spencer W. Kimball ushered in a new era of missionary work when he proclaimed:

"When I ask for more missionaries, I am not asking for more testimony-barren or unworthy missionaries. I am asking that we . . . train our missionaries better in every branch and every ward . . . that [our] young people will understand that it is a great privilege to go on a mission and that they must be physically well, mentally well, spiritually well, and that 'the Lord cannot look upon sin with the least degree of allowance.'

"[We are] asking for missionaries who have been carefully . . . trained through the family and the organizations of the Church, and who come . . . with a great desire" ("When the World Will Be Converted," *Ensign,* Oct. 1974, 7).

And further: "We must prepare our [young] missionaries better, not only with language but with scripture and above all with a testimony and a burning fire that puts power to their words" (address delivered at Regional Representatives' seminar, 5 Apr. 1976, 14).

To serve the Lord as a full-time missionary is a privilege; the primary purpose of full-time missionary service is the building up of the kingdom of God. And the Lord needs his best. Young men and young women who respond to the call must be prepared for the most rigorous challenge of their young lives—prepared spiritually, intellectually, emotionally, and physically.

Although our missionaries are strengthened, elevated, and magnified by their service, that is not their primary purpose, and neither they nor their families nor their leaders should regard a mission as the solution to unresolved problems. The Lord needs our best; he needs those who can run—not just walk, but run—physically and spiritually, those who can wield eternal influence with purity and strength and conviction.

Does this mean that those who are not yet ready should be turned away or rejected? Of course not! It means that our young people, their families, and their leaders should each accept the personal responsibility for preparing worthy, able, and committed volunteers for the Lord's royal army.

As we shoulder this great responsibility, the Lord will magnify our efforts and he will magnify our missionaries. They will become the instruments through which he will perform his miracles.

In 1980 President Kimball urged that "every family, every night and every morning, . . . pray to the Lord to open the doors of other nations so that their people, too, may have the gospel of Jesus Christ" (*The Teachings of Spencer W. Kimball,* ed. Edward L. Kimball [Salt Lake City: Bookcraft, 1982], 586). During the past few years we have seen the fruition of his vision.

In 1989, during the brief period of weeks, we witnessed some phenomenal changes in the world, particularly in the Eastern bloc countries, changes that God-fearing people attribute to the hand of the Almighty in bringing about his glorious purposes to fill the earth with the knowledge of the Lord. Walls came down, gates opened, and millions of voices cho-rused the song of freedom. We rejoice in the dawning of a brighter day.

The news media made the events in eastern Europe appear as purely political revolutions, even though many of the oppressed have recognized it as a "religious renaissance" and have acknowledged the influence of divine intervention (*USA Today,* 16 Mar. 1990).

A prominent national magazine editorialized on the reasons for this sudden, dramatic change. It was "an idea—. . . democracy—and its phe-nomenally successful application in America" and some other parts of the world. The article concluded: "America's contribution to the world will continue to be in the realm of ideas and ideals" ("An American Vision for the 1990s," *Fortune,* 26 Mar. 1990, 14).

The peoples in eastern Europe have slowly but effectively been exposed to ideals of truth and basic rights through messages by satellite, radio, printed materials, even programs and recordings of the Mormon Tabernacle Choir, word of mouth, heart-to-heart contacts, and the light of Christ encouraging seeds of truth to seep into their consciousness—a pre-cept here and a precept there. And when the opportunity arrived, they confidently seized upon it.

The transformation of once-mighty man-made empires with such speed and determination released new springs of faith and hope in the hearts of hundreds of millions of oppressed souls. Where there was despair, now the bright light of freedom shines forth. This could have hap-pened in such a miraculous way only by the intervening hand of the Almighty. "Is any thing too hard for the Lord?" (Genesis 18:14).

The Bible is replete with admonitions to remember the mighty acts of God as he has intervened in history for his people. We are witnesses of his mighty, intervening hand in the world even today.

President Joseph F. Smith declared: "The Almighty raised up [America] by the power of his omnipotent hand, that it might be possible in the latter days for the kingdom of God to be established in the earth. . . . His hand has been over this nation, and it is his purpose and design to enlarge it, make it glorious . . . to the end that those who are kept in bondage and serfdom may be brought to the enjoyment of the fullest freedom and liberty of conscience possible for intelligent men to exercise in the earth" (*Gospel Doctrine* [Salt Lake City: Deseret Book, 1939], 409).

The religious freedom established in America made possible the coming forth of the plain and precious truths of the Book of Mormon "to the convincing of the Jew and Gentile that JESUS is the CHRIST, the ETERNAL GOD, manifesting himself unto all nations" (Preface to the Book of Mormon). These writings are to come unto the Gentiles that they may "know the decrees of God" and repent (Ether 2:11).

It is incumbent upon the members of the Church who have had the gift of religious freedom to share this knowledge and testimony with the peoples of the world. Do not underestimate the profound influence—politically and socially—of the principles of the restored gospel upon all of mankind.

The opportunity for meaningful service to others is expanding rapidly. To some of us, it's just across the street; to others, across the ocean. The destiny of many nations is now being decided. Every generation is crucial. We may not be responsible for past generations, but we cannot escape the responsibility for this present one. It is beyond our comprehension to imagine the billions of souls who depend upon us to bring them—some way, somehow—this glorious message of the gospel. Of course, not all people will accept, but all must be given the opportunity to hear and respond after being taught by the Spirit of Christ.

We declare in all solemnity that the Lord is now preparing the nations of the earth to receive the truth he desires them to have. But in order for a person to accept the truth, he must prepare himself by exercising faith in the Lord and Savior, Jesus Christ. Such faith accepts the existence of God our Father, the teachings of Jesus concerning man's dealings with his fellowmen, and the teachings concerning Christ's relationship to God as his Son. Once a person has prepared himself to receive and accept truth, it is then sealed upon his heart by the power of the Holy Ghost, who is the Testifier of Truth. It is then incumbent upon him to so conform his life to those standards of truth. This may require fundamental changes in lifestyle and the seeking of repentance for sins committed.

The Lord's power is at hand and evident. True believers will have unusual opportunities to be of service. I am convinced that those who labor unselfishly in behalf of others, with no thought of remuneration, will be physically and spiritually refreshed and renewed. We must prove ourselves, have the desire, and be found worthy to assist the Lord in accomplishing his purposes with men on earth.

The Lord instructed his young prophet, Joseph, in October 1831: "The keys of the kingdom of God are committed unto man on the earth, and from thence shall the gospel roll forth unto the ends of the earth, as the stone which is cut out of the mountain without hands shall roll forth, until it has filled the whole earth" (D&C 65:2).

I testify we are witnessing the fulfillment of this promise, and that this work, given by Almighty God to his Son to proclaim, to teach, and finally to judge, will be done with eternal love.

11

LOVE, THE KEY TO CONVERSION

harity, or the pure love of Christ, is the greatest and most powerful motive in spreading the gospel. "A new commandment I give
unto you," said the Savior, "that ye love one another, as I have
loved you" (John 13:34).

A man "must needs have charity," Mormon taught, or "he is nothing"
(Moroni 7:44). Charity is especially important in missionary work. Its
influence, radiated by the missionary, helps to create within the investiga-
tor a desire to learn and softens his heart to the truth. Charity can fill the
missionary with an unquenchable desire to serve his fellowmen. Without
it, as difficulties arise and proselyting seems unfruitful, he may lose interest and slacken his pace. But with Christlike love, the missionary will persevere through adversity because he becomes a caring and dutiful
messenger of Christ. A Christlike love for others can purify a missionary's
motives and consecrate his labor and true desire to share the gospel.

Recently, a university professor in California found the Church. He
had been taught by many sets of missionaries over a long period of time.
Why did he finally see the light? He replied, "I felt the love of Christ
through this team of new missionaries. As they taught me, I understood."

While Sister Haight and I were in Japan, the mission president told us about a new convert to the Church who, when the missionaries came to her door, started to cry. Asked why, she told about being in the hospital, where she was seriously ill, and one night she couldn't sleep. Her grandfather, who had been dead many years, appeared to her and told her that "two young men in Western clothes with a strange new book will come. Listen! Be kind! The message is true!"

The Prophet Joseph Smith taught: "It is a time-honored adage that love begets love. Let us pour forth love—show forth everlasting increase; cast our bread upon the waters and we shall receive it after many days, increased to a hundredfold. Friendship," he continued, "is like Brother Turley in his blacksmith shop welding iron to iron; it unites the human family with its happy influence" (*Teachings of the Prophet Joseph Smith*, sel. Joseph Fielding Smith [Salt Lake City: Deseret Book, 1938], 316).

The story is told about a family from Southern California who, while on a vacation, passed through St. George, Utah. They hadn't been there before, and the man, who had some interest in architecture, was intrigued by the St. George Temple. He parked the car by the temple and got out and walked around the building, along with his wife and their two little girls. Finally the parents went into the visitors center at the temple, and the two girls went across the street to sit in the shade of a tree on the lawn of a Latter-day Saint meetinghouse.

Primary was about to start, and the Primary teacher came out and rounded up all of the children and asked them to come in to Primary. Seeing those two strange girls, she said, "Come on in to Primary." The girls went in.

When the parents came out of the visitors center about an hour later, they couldn't find their children. They looked and searched, and the father, anxious to get on his way, was becoming a little upset. Finally he saw his daughters coming out of the building across the street. "Where have you been?" he asked them.

"We've been to Primary," said the girls.

"Primary? What's Primary?"

"Primary, Daddy, is where they teach about Jesus. And besides that, you shouldn't be smoking." He almost swallowed the cigar that he had in his mouth.

He said, "Come on and get in the car. Let's be on our way."

And the little girls said, "We can't go."

"We can't go? Why not?"

They said, "We're in a play."

"A play?"

"Yes, Daddy, we're in a play, and we have to stay all week and rehearse."

The family stayed all week and rehearsed, two Latter-day Saint missionaries met them, and they were all baptized. Why? Because of the love they found in the Church.

Hollywood would never be able to produce the thrilling stories, the real-life dramas, the diaries, the letters home, the testimonies locked in hearts that have resulted from following the Savior's instruction: "Go ye therefore, and teach all nations, baptizing them in the name of the Father, and of the Son, and of the Holy Ghost" (Matthew 28:19). The Savior explained what might happen to some of our efforts. He said: "A sower went out to sow his seed: and as he sowed, some fell by the way side; and it was trodden down, . . . and some fell upon a rock; and as soon as it was sprung up, it withered away. . . . and other fell on good ground, and sprang up, and bare fruit an hundredfold" (Luke 8:5–6, 8). Imagine the quantity of seed planted over the years by the tens of thousands of missionaries. Some seeds lie dormant for years—others spring forth immediately. Some years ago such a precious seed was planted in fertile soil in Germany.

Robert Frederick Lippolt, his wife, and their daughters lived in a small city in central Germany. One Sunday, while Robert's wife was on her way to the Protestant church, she was approached by Latter-day Saint missionaries, who invited her to attend sacrament meeting. She attended and was impressed. After subsequent visits to her home by the missionaries, she was baptized and became active in the Church. From the moment of his wife's baptism, the husband grew bitter toward the Church. Their daughters were also baptized, resulting in more bitterness.

Robert could bear the Mormons no longer; he moved his family from Germany to Vera Cruz, Mexico, and then on to Porto Alegre, Brazil. As soon as they were settled, his wife continued to spread the news of the gospel. She caused excitement in Brazil, for the doctrine she preached was completely new. Bitterness filled Robert. He hated the Mormons. He refused to let his children go to public schools for fear they would learn to read and would thus be further indoctrinated with Mormon literature. Finally, in desperation, he took his family away from civilization to the interior of Brazil. They settled in the remote, peaceful valley of Ipomeia in the state of Santa Catarina.

Filled with a burning testimony and a desire to share the "good news," Robert's faithful wife wrote to the mission president in Germany, who in turn referred her to the Argentine Mission president. She asked that he visit Brazil. President Reinhold Stoof visited Brazil in 1927 and reported that much success could be realized among the German-speaking people of Brazil. From the tiny seeds sown by missionaries in Germany and carried across the Atlantic, the First Presidency established a mission in Brazil in February 1935. The work flourished. Hundreds and then thousands heard the good news.

Even Robert Frederick Lippolt, the once-bitter husband and father, was eventually touched by the seed of truth, for at the age of eighty-three he was carried in his wooden rocking chair to the nearby River Rio de Peixe and was baptized a member of The Church of Jesus Christ of Latter-day Saints. How could one ever describe the deep, abiding love of Robert's faithful wife for the gospel and for her family?

We have been a missionary church from the beginning. I thank the Lord that we will always be a missionary church. The first conversions in this dispensation came through the humble testimony of the Prophet Joseph Smith. His efforts were directed first to those he loved most. He converted his father, his mother, and his brothers and sisters. He converted his wife, his neighbors, then Martin Harris, and the schoolteacher, Oliver Cowdery, as well as the Whitmer family. They all felt of the truth and power of his simple testimony:

"On Sunday, 11 April 1830, Oliver Cowdery preached the first public discourse that was delivered by any of our number," wrote the Prophet. Then it was recorded that six were baptized following the service.

Joseph Smith and Oliver Cowdery, under divine instruction, began to preach, teach, expound, exhort, and baptize and to set the pattern for our modern missionary service. Now, more than 150 years later, we see the fruits of missionary efforts in our own families, in our wards and branches, and in the stakes and missions throughout the world.

The gospel of Jesus Christ is the hope and everlasting salvation for all mankind. Our young people should be reared under the loving guidance and influence of good homes—homes where the blessing of a mission is part of their life's goal, homes where plans for a future mission become part of their lives.

People are exposed to the gospel in interesting ways. President Lawrence R. Flake, who was the mission president in Independence, Missouri, told me about meeting a man on an airplane. As they were seated and having a little conversation on the plane, the stranger asked President Flake, "What is your business?" President Flake said, "Well, I'm in an interesting business. I have a hundred and sixty young college students who work for me for nothing." This man said, "I'm interested in that. Can you tell me more about it?" He developed an interest right away.

A few years ago I was on an airplane, and after I had sat down, a flight attendant came along. It was a warm day and she had a tray of cool drinks. She stood and looked at me for a moment, then asked, "What would you like?"

"Do you have a Seven-Up?"

"Yes." As she handed it to me, she said, "What is on that tie pin you're wearing?"

I have a little pin that has the emblem of the London Temple on it, so I said, "That's a temple."

"A temple? A temple of what?"

"That's the temple of the Lord."

Then she asked, "What church do you belong to?"

I told her, "I belong to The Church of Jesus Christ of Latter-day Saints—the Mormon church."

She said, "After I get through passing out these drinks, could I come and talk to you?"

I replied, "I'd be happy to talk with you."

When she came back later, she knelt in the aisle beside me, looked into my face, and said, "I saw you when you came on the plane, and when you sat down in this seat I had a feeling that I needed to get acquainted with you. Then I saw that tie pin. Could you tell me a little bit about your church?"

I told her briefly that this was the only true church on the face of the earth. And then I asked, "Are you married?"

"No."

"Do you have a steady boyfriend?"

"No."

I said, "I'm impressed to make you a promise. If you'll give me your name and address, I will have somebody come and tell you about this temple. The promise I want to make is that if you will listen, and do what they ask you to do, you'll find a young man who will marry you in one of these temples."

She said, "Just a minute while I get a paper and pencil." She came back and handed me a piece of paper on which she had written her name, Penny Harriman, and her address.

Months later I received a telephone call. The voice at the other end said, "My name is Penny Harriman. Do you remember me?"

"Yes, I remember you."

"Would you perform a wedding for us in the Salt Lake Temple?"

And I said, "I'd be thrilled to."

When I entered the special room in the temple, the young man had many of his family and friends seated on one side. Penny was alone; none of her family belonged to the Church. I said, "Penny, before we begin, why don't you tell how we met?" She told this story and how she had had a feeling in her heart that she should talk to me.

There is something unusual about this work. It is special. But we have to live for it, and we have to develop a life pattern so that the gospel becomes a part of it.

The message we take to the world through our missionary efforts is divine and must be accepted by all people if they are to be saved. Our message is

1. That Jesus Christ is the Son of God, the Redeemer of the world.

2. That Joseph Smith was the instrument, the prophet, prepared to reveal the knowledge of Christ and the plan of salvation in this dispensation.

3. That The Church of Jesus Christ of Latter-day Saints is the only true and living Church upon the face of the whole earth.

The message is true. Millions of God's children are waiting to hear it. May we accept the challenge and show our love for our fellowmen by increasing our efforts to find and teach them.

12

A Challenge for Future Missionaries

While I was attending a regional conference in Mesa, Arizona, several years ago, a young girl of about nine or ten years of age handed me a letter and asked if I would please give it to President Ezra Taft Benson, who was then president of the Church. I said, "Of course I will." As I read the letter, written in her childish handwriting, I was touched by her simple, direct, but unquestioned testimony. Let me read it to you:

"Dear President Benson:

"My name is Megan Freestone and I wanted you to know that I love you as a great leader of the Church and as my brother in Christ.

"I would like to bear my testimony to you that I know that this Church is the true and living Church on earth and that Jesus Christ is the head of this Church and I know that you lead the Church under him.

"I love my family. I love you. I love all my brothers and sisters all around the world, and I love my Savior.

"I have a witness and testimony that the Book of Mormon is the word of God and that if I follow God's word I will make it back home to live with my Father again.

"Again, I love you and my prayers are with you and all the leaders of this Church. And I know that you love me. All my love, Megan."

How beautiful, plain, and simple are these words of a sweet child—but how powerful the message.

Another powerful message was delivered in the prayer of a six-year-old Primary girl. The Sharing Time presentation had centered on how careful planning makes things run smoothly and peacefully in our lives, and then it related this to God's plan of salvation for us. The little girl stood at the close of Primary and said:

"Dear Heavenly Father, Help us to plan better so we can be happier. I love you. In the name of Jesus Christ, amen."

How wonderful and refreshing are the humble, unrehearsed words of children. How many of us tell Heavenly Father that we love him? Or do we feel that we have outgrown the need for simple expressions of love and appreciation to our Creator, or that we are too sophisticated for such emotions and feelings? We might all learn great lessons from the children around us.

I am a witness of miracles from our Savior in guiding this work. I have been associated with thousands of faithful young men and women who have diligently prepared themselves to serve a mission, with wonderful results.

In 1839 the Quorum of the Twelve Apostles, with Brigham Young as president of the Quorum, mailed out an epistle that was addressed "To the Elders of the Church of Jesus Christ of Latter-day Saints, to the Churches Scattered Abroad and to All the Saints."

The epistle was directed particularly to "the elders"—or those called and ordained to proclaim the gospel of Jesus Christ to the world. Sisters had not been called at that time, but I believe that these words are addressed just as well to them. I quote those stirring words written by those called and trained and schooled by the Prophet Joseph himself:

"We would say to the Elders, that God has called you to an important office. He has laid upon you an onerous duty; He has called you to an holy calling, even to be the priests of the Most High God, messengers to the nations of the earth; and upon your diligence, your perseverance and faithfulness, . . . hang the destinies of the human family. You are [those whom] God has called to spread forth His kingdom. He has committed the care of souls to your charge, and when you received this [calling] you became the [official emissaries] of heaven, and the Great God demands it of you, that you should be faithful" (*History of The Church of Jesus Christ of Latter-day Saints,* ed. B. H. Roberts, 2d ed. rev., 7 vols. [Salt Lake City: The Church of Jesus Christ of Latter-day Saints, 1932–51], 3:395).

The message we have been given to proclaim is the grandest in all the world. The proclaiming of this message is not merely the most important work in the world; we, with our knowledge, say it is the very reason the world was created. There is no loftier work than to teach inspired words that change lives and bring happiness and even transformation in personalities as we assist our Savior Jesus Christ in bringing to pass the eternal life of man.

Many years ago a best-selling book about the noble and courageous people who conquered the western areas of the United States was entitled *Men to Match My Mountains.*

The Lord needs "messengers to match his message!" He needs each of us to be the messenger able to wield the powerful message that he has placed in our hands. I would hope that we are serious in our commitment to want to further the work of the Lord, that we will prepare ourselves spiritually and physically to be able to be the kind of messenger required in this period of uncertainty in much of the world, to bring the gospel of salvation into the lives of those who may have lost hope and who are wondering, "Have we heard all there is to hear? There must be more—a clearer message to lift our souls."

In a letter dated 4 March 1993, the First Presidency emphasized that "Full-time missionary service is not a right, but a privilege . . . [That] Missionary service is for the benefit of the Lord and His Church to fulfill His purposes." The letter then went on to reemphasize the importance of preparing worthy, qualified individuals for the sacred responsibility of missionary service.

The responsibility for that preparation lies, first of all, with each individual young person. Each one should ask himself or herself, Am I doing all in my power to keep myself clean and pure before the Lord, or have I allowed myself to be beguiled by the adversary's lie that I can "eat, drink, and be merry; . . . there is no harm in this; . . . and if it so be that [I am] guilty, God will beat [me] with a few stripes," and then all will be well? (2 Nephi 28:8). How can we believe that we can sin for a season, with the intention of eventually repenting, and still go forth to effectively proclaim the gospel of repentance?

Such individuals do not realize the price that may be asked of them in order to resolve those "innocent sins." Those who think they can bring their lives back into order merely by desisting for a period of time from certain activities (which they really would rather indulge in, if they could have their own way) betray a lack of understanding of gospel principles and a superficial faith in the Lord. They are confusing *refraining* for true *repenting*.

We need young men and women who are willing to set aside the things that may have filled their lives thus far—in the apostle Paul's words, to put away "childish things" and become strong individuals (1 Corinthians 13:11). We need individuals today who are willing to withstand the immoral influences of the world and to commit themselves to hard work, individuals who are willing to stretch themselves beyond even the best that they have ever done before and to change the rest of their lives in the process.

The lives of many are filled with a variety of wants and desires and interests and pursuits: family, friends, school, sports, music, hiking, clothes, television, movies, cars, Church activities, food, reading, and so on. For each, the menu may be a little different, but for most it will be fairly long. This diversity of interests is part of what makes our lives so rich and rewarding.

Some of those things may be good and positive, perhaps among the most enduring and rewarding things in a person's life. Others may be neither good nor bad, depending on the use they are put to. Moreover, I presume that most of us have had at least a few things in our lives that were not so good, perhaps a few bad habits or personal weaknesses, or perhaps a transgression that has needed to be resolved through the bishop or stake president—but that causes us to repent and change.

As young people prepare themselves to serve the Lord, we hope that they are beginning to realize that there are things to do with their time and energy beyond those things that give them just personal pleasure. We hope that they are in the process of correcting wrongs and strengthening the moral fibers of their character through thorough soul-searching and repentance, if necessary. We hope that they are beginning to concentrate their efforts toward building a store of knowledge through scripture reading, study, and service to someone else, and that they are really learning the power and blessings of personal progress that will benefit them throughout their lives and that will help lift and inspire others.

Have you ever noticed that any individual who yearns to excel in any field undergoes a radical simplification of his or her focus? Take the young person dedicated to becoming a concert pianist. How many hours each day does he practice? How much time is left for all the things with which you and I fill our lives, many of which are trivial or unessential?

Take the student who is dedicated to winning a highly prestigious scholarship. How much time and energy is committed to this goal? How much is left over for other things?

Take the young girl who yearns to become an Olympic figure skater. Where is she every morning at four or five o'clock? Of course, down at the skating rink. Then she dashes off to school, but as soon as school is over, she's right back at the rink—a break for dinner, and then either back to the rink or some time for school work. How diverse, how complicated has her life become? It has been pared down to just a few essentials. All else has been sacrificed for the cause, for the lofty goal that is her life's central focus.

Focus is the key word. And that focus has been won through a lot of discipline and hard work.

When any individual pays that sort of price—when any of us sacrifices to achieve that sort of discipline and focus in our lives—there is some pain and suffering, but there is a pay-back, and we see it in the tremendous growth, the lofty level of excellence that such people attain. How many of us in those rare moments of insight can taste just a bit of the yearning desire that is the source of their sacrificing, their commitment, their focus?

As individuals accept calls to serve in the mission field, they are asked to leave behind most of those desires and yearnings and interest that filled their lives before. They will take with them their scriptures, their gosepl knowledge, and their testimony—and little else. The good, the bad, the indifferent—everything—will be left behind as they begin to experience that sharpening of focus that is usually the experience only of those few who have committed themselves to excellence in their chosen pursuits.

As they experience this refining of their focus, they can begin to understand what the prophets have recorded when they have written about giving all our heart, might, and mind to the Lord, when they have written about singleness of heart and of mind.

"Thou shalt love the Lord thy God with all thy heart, and with all thy soul, and with all thy mind" (Matthew 22:37).

"Blessed are they that keep his testimonies, and that seek him with the whole heart" (Psalm 119:2).

"I would that ye should come unto Christ, who is the Holy One of Israel, and partake of his salvation, and the power of his redemption. Yea, come unto him, and offer your whole souls as an offering unto him, . . . and as the Lord liveth ye will be saved" (Omni 1:26).

Does that sound rather all consuming? Well, how about these words:

"No man can serve two masters: for either he will hate the one, and love the other; or else he will hold to the one, and despise the other. Ye cannot serve God and mammon" (Matthew 6:24).

And finally, that rather high and hard standard the Lord himself set for those who would embark on his service: "No man, having put his hand to the plough, and looking back, is fit for the kingdom of God" (Luke 9:62).

Do you catch something of the vision of what the Lord expects of us? Does that vision seem somewhat intimidating? Or can you glimpse the way in which it can liberate us from the shackles of the world?

Latter-day Saints are among the good, the worthy, the honorable of the earth—among the best that dwells on the earth at this time. But to become a mighty instrument of the Lord's power takes unusual discipline—the discipline of the committed, dedicated scholar, musician, or athlete—and even more!

No one has ever said that a mission is easy. If they did, they weren't telling the whole truth. During the eighteen months or two years that missionaries serve, they are likely to face more opposition than ever before in their lives. That's part of the plan that each of us sustained and accepted. In the book of Abraham we read: "And there stood one among them that was like unto God, and he said unto those who were with him: We will go down, for there is space there, and we will take of these materials, and we will make an earth whereon these may dwell; and *we will prove them herewith,* to see if they will do *all* things whatsoever the Lord their God shall command them" (Abraham 3:24–25; emphasis added).

We are in the midst of a test. We are being proved, to see whether we will do *all things* that the Lord asks of us. Why is it so important that we be proved, tried, and tested? Partly, of course, to indicate to the Lord, and prove to ourselves, that the eternal reward we will receive is justified. It is but part of the price that must be paid for the heavenly rewards that lie in store.

But perhaps even more important is this principle: through the trying and the testing we are refined and purified and strengthened and magnified, just as a metal is purified and tempered in the refiner's fire.

The numerous challenges the Prophet Joseph faced all of his life strengthened and prepared him for his ultimate destiny. The tremendous faith and courage of the early Brethren called to missions in Europe—England, Italy, Denmark, and Sweden—enabled the newly established Church to gain a strong foothold. Imagine the faith and testimony of young Samuel Smith, the first missionary in this dispensation, that allowed him to set out with only his testimony of the restored gospel and the divine calling of the Prophet Joseph, and a Book of Mormon under his arm!

Serving a mission may be one of the greatest experiences of a person's life, but part of the reason for that will be the opposition the missionary may face and struggle with and overcome. But please rest assured, this will be for his or her good, and none of us will ever need to face that opposition alone as long as we do not move away from the Lord. Whom the Lord calls, he will magnify.

These are challenging opportunities. But the challenge pales in comparison to one of the most beautiful promises in all the scriptures: "And if your eye be single to my glory, your whole bodies shall be filled with light, and there shall be no darkness in you; and that body which is filled with light comprehendeth all things. Therefore, sanctify yourselves that your minds become single to God, and the days will come that you shall see him; for he will unveil his face unto you, and it shall be in his own time, and in his own way, and according to his own will" (D&C 88:67–68).

There is much work to be done. We need many more laborers in the vineyard. We need to make our work more effective and productive. We need to better prepare ourselves to not only sow the seeds of the gospel of Jesus Christ, but to reap the harvest of more solid, faithful members.

The Lord has entrusted the salvation of the souls of people into our hands. President Spencer W. Kimball said: "Please do not confuse this straightforward emphasis on missionary work with mere statistics. Our concerns are with souls, not statistics. We desire growth only because that will mean that we are reaching our Father's children who desperately need the gospel and Church in their lives. . . . What we have been doing in our missionary efforts is good, but it is not good enough. It is time to stir ourselves, and then we can stir others" (mission presidents' seminar, June 1979).

I encourage all Latter-day Saints everywhere to study the Book of Mormon and other scriptures, to be diligent in their prayers, to bear their testimonies often, to develop sensitivity to the Spirit and the faith to follow the promptings of that Holy Spirit, and to experience the effects of Christ's atonement in their own lives.

13

A CHALLENGE FOR
OLDER COUPLES

A few years ago Sister Haight and I drove along the coast of Chile with one of the mission presidents in that country. In large cities and small villages, we saw the fruits of our missionary proselyting efforts. We met with many new members and were deeply impressed with their faith and humble desire to learn more about the gospel they have accepted. As we continued the journey, our concern centered on ways we could help this growing number of new members to increase and strengthen their faith so they could hold on to the iron rod and continue to grow in knowledge. We reflected on the many priesthood, Relief Society, and Sunday School classes back home attended by husbands and wives trained in the gospel, many of them with unusual talents not now being used. Many stakes are crowded with mature couples fully prepared to accept a mission call, couples who could enthusiastically help not only in spreading the gospel but also in strengthening new members in areas of the world where we are growing so rapidly.

The thousands of newly baptized members, now in a new church that has somewhat unfamiliar ways, might be encouraged and trained by people who today are sitting comfortably at home. We thought, if only we could transplant hundreds of our faithful, well-prepared couples out into one of the greatest chapters of their lives! Amulek taught concerning the Savior, "He shall come into the world to redeem his people" (Alma 11:40). Should we not encourage "his people" and help prepare them for his coming?

Many Latter-day Saints think of full-time missionary service as being suitable only for young single men and women; however, a new social pattern is emerging in our society: the number of men and women retiring from active employment or professions is continually increasing. Many of them are healthy and vigorous, ready for new challenges.

Some time ago I received a query from friends in California. The husband was retiring from schoolteaching and indicated a desire to return to Utah. He asked, "What can we do for the Church when we return?" My answer was, "Don't come to Utah. Your Church experience is needed out in the world. Brush up on the Norwegian you learned as a missionary years ago." They were soon on their way to the mission field. He was thrilled with this opportunity to serve a second mission, this time with the additional blessing of having the same companion for his entire mission.

Many couples are prepared and waiting for their bishop to extend a mission call. Perhaps the bishop, busy with other duties, has overlooked them. Those who desire to serve the Lord need not wait for the bishop but should knock on his door and say, "We feel we are ready to go."

Several years ago, President Spencer W. Kimball announced:

"We could use hundreds of couples, older people like some of you folks, whose families are reared, who have retired in their business, who are able to go and spend their own money, to teach the gospel. We could use hundreds of couples. You just go and talk to your bishop," he continued, "that is all you need to do. Tell him, 'We are ready to go, if you can use us.' I think you will probably get a call" (*The Teachings of Spencer W. Kimball,* ed. Edward L. Kimball [Salt Lake City: Bookcraft, 1982], 551).

Since President Kimball made that plea, the demand has continued to increase, and today we could use not only hundreds but thousands of prepared couples.

There are many hundreds of experienced, devoted couples—those whose hair may be graying and perhaps with a wrinkle here or there—you know, those distinguishing features of maturity—that are retiring from their professional careers but with several productive years still remaining before their golden years, whose children have made lives of their own, who are in good health, and who dream of that eventful moment when they say to their bishop, "We're ready—ready to do something really important—to go on a mission, to go anywhere the Lord needs us."

Such was the situation of Hollis and Gwen Kersey, who sold their home, bought a little farm, fixed up the house to be warm and comfortable, cleared the land, and planted a garden. "We settled down to be retired," they said. They were Baptists and had no thought of changing religions this late in life. But missionaries and a neighbor family touched their lives, and they were baptized. On their fortieth wedding anniversary they were sealed in the Atlanta Temple. They were soon called as stake missionaries and later called to serve a full-time mission.

As they arrived at the Missionary Training Center, the Kerseys remarked: "We gave away the chickens, turkeys, rabbits, took the pony and two dogs . . . [to our] son, . . . emptied the freezers and gave away the cats, . . . boarded up the windows, nailed up the sheds, had everything turned off, went and kissed our ten grandchildren good-bye and here we are!"

What a marvelous attitude!

In Mexico I had the opportunity of meeting a wonderful, mature missionary couple, Brother and Sister John Fossum, who commented: "Our great need is for trained leadership. Married couples with years of experience in Church work could literally work miracles. We have twenty-two scattered branches but have not been able to adequately train the branch leaders. We are growing so rapidly that leaders with experience are not available."

The Fossums continued: "Many blessings have come to us as a result of our mission, blessings we receive from the Lord whenever we serve without restraint. Some people shrivel up and die in beds and rocking chairs. We didn't want that kind of retirement. The Lord knew we wanted to go on a mission—and we received a call. Some couples imagine they can't live without their families close by, and some fear for their own physical well-being. It was reassuring when our stake president set us apart; he promised us that the Lord would look after our family and that we would have good health to the end of our mission. At our age it's difficult to live up to missionary schedules, but we have found it's possible, and it has its rewards."

Brother Fossum told me, "Fifty years ago I served a mission in Hawaii and learned to speak Hawaiian. It was difficult then, and it was difficult at our age now to go through the Missionary Training Center and learn Spanish, but we did it. It has been a great learning experience. The spiritual treasures alone are worth the effort." Sister Fossum added, "It's really hard on a grandmother to be away from twenty-six grandchildren, but I'm coming through with flying colors—sometimes at half-mast but always flying." Then this dedicated couple concluded, "A mission for those of mature years is a rich, rewarding experience. It is for those who want to live out their retirement and not just exist."

We need more—many more—couples like the Fossums, people who are willing, wondering, and asking, "What can I do for the Lord?" We need couples who are willing to use part of their golden years in the Lord's vital service.

In the early days of the Church, the Lord's work urgently required the sacrifice and best efforts of the Saints. A company of brethren commanded to leave their families and go to Missouri in 1831 were admonished: "Wherefore, be not weary in well-doing, for ye are laying the foundation of a great work. And out of small things proceedeth that which is great. Behold, the Lord requireth the heart and a willing mind; and the willing and obedient shall eat the good of the land of Zion in these last days" (D&C 64:33–34).

To every married couple, I would say: Don't wait until your retirement dinner and the traditional gold watch to make plans, but start now. Prepare for what may be the most rewarding experience of your life. Begin now to expand your horizons, to increase your knowledge. Why not learn another language? You might start with Spanish or German. My wife, Ruby, after a fifty-year lapse, returned to the university to take Spanish

101. Hard work? Of course! Long hours of study to keep up? Many. Who does the cooking? Sometimes I do. Rewarding? I am very proud of her when she bears a humble testimony that our members in Argentina or Mexico can understand.

We are witnessing a continuing unfolding of the Lord's work in this, the last dispensation. Millions are waiting and want to improve their lives. The Lord will bless us if we ask in faith. Mature couples are needed everywhere, particularly experienced members with family ties to other lands. A spiritual rebirth can be theirs as they serve the Lord in total service. Prayer will have a deeper dimension. Scriptures will be pondered and more deeply appreciated. The Holy Ghost will become more evident. Their capacity to love will increase. Their families at home will be blessed.

Moroni, the Book of Mormon prophet, taught about the careful attention given the newly baptized person in his day: "After they had been received unto baptism, and were wrought upon and cleansed by the power of the Holy Ghost, they were numbered among the people of the Church of Christ; and their names were taken, that they might be remembered and nourished by the good word of God, to keep them in the right way, to keep them continually watchful unto prayer" (Moroni 6:4). In many areas of the world, we have converts who need to be remembered with care and love, who need to be encouraged and kept in the right way, as Moroni stated. But the couples with experience usually live elsewhere. We need the help of seasoned members who can provide training, encouragement, and, above all, compassionate concern.

To show what can be accomplished with such love and dedication, let me share with you again the words of Brother and Sister Fossum: "To visit one of our branches, we get up at 4:00 A.M. on Sunday to catch an early bus. Sister Fossum started a little music class for the sisters and taught them the basics of directing music. One thirteen-year-old girl with a perfect sense of time now leads the singing in sacrament meeting.

"I was invited to attend their branch presidency meeting," Brother Fossum continued, "to show how we do some things. A few months ago in this branch, home teaching and visiting teaching were just words in a book, but now nine pairs of home teachers are making their visits, and visiting teachers will soon be organized. But these are incidental rewards. The great rewards come when the service we give and the love we feel for the humble members result in a change in their lives for the better. Then we too are enriched."

While firefighters were battling roaring forest fires in the West a few years ago, two grandmothers—Altha Clark, from Texas, and Hazel Stills, from Florida—kindled countless spiritual flames by creating new "interest in people who [had] investigated the Church for years, but who needed a firm, loving nudge to accept baptism," and, with caring fellowshipping, reached out to the less-active members.

"They don't take no for an answer," the second counselor in the Altamont Utah Stake presidency said, "and they [teach] without offending anyone." A rancher said the two sisters "have kept us so busy I don't have time to get my hay in. We . . . keep them [booked with people] to teach. In this stake, the full-time missionaries teach very few discussions without a stake missionary or fellowshipper going along."

The two grandmothers traveled about one hundred miles a day on unpaved country roads, and the dust and ruts didn't slow them down. While visiting a member's home, these remarkable missionaries asked if she knew someone they could teach. The sister replied, "My husband." Directed by the Spirit how to approach this husband, they taught him the gospel and rejoiced with his wife at his baptism.

Fourteen families became active and went to the temple because of the efforts of these full-time grandmother missionaries coordinating with the stake missionaries and properly following a plan in fellowshipping new members (*Church News*, 10 Sept. 1988, 8, 9, 12).

When people are taught and then fellowshipped with warmth and continued interest until they are integrated into the mainstream of the Church, they are "remembered and nourished by the good word of God, to keep them in the right way" (Moroni 6:4). By working together, stake missionaries and full-time missionaries are able to keep new converts involved as they gain gospel knowledge and a needed testimony. They are also bringing back into fellowship less-active members.

In stressing the need for mature men and women to be about the work of the Lord, President Benson related the experience of his two widowed sisters. One was the mother of ten children and the other the mother of eight. After they had sent their children on missions, they approached their bishops about going on missions themselves. President Benson related that he remembered well the day a number of years ago when they called him and said, "Guess what? We've received our missionary calls." President Benson said, "What missionary calls?" And they replied, "We're both going to your old field of labor in England" ("Our Commission to Take the Gospel to All the World," *Ensign,* May 1984, 45).

They did go to England and served as companions for twenty months.

Thousands of devoted mature couples and single sisters have touched the lives of many for good. We are grateful for their dedication and courage and oftentimes great personal sacrifice. One couple indicated on their missionary form that they would be ready to go just as soon as they were able to find a home for their eighty hives of bees.

There is an unusual opportunity for qualified individuals to do their utmost to fulfill the Lord's injunction to preach his gospel to the ends of the earth and not only to *teach* but *convert,* as Alma said, that as many "as believed in their preaching, and were converted unto the Lord, never did fall away" (Alma 23:6).

The Lord instructed in the Doctrine and Covenants, "If ye have desires to serve God ye are called to the work" (D&C 4:3). Many undoubtedly have the desire but may need some gentle encouragement to complete their decision.

I challenged eight couples in my former home stake in California to set aside their comfortable lives of planned retirement and to bless the Scottish Saints with their gospel knowledge and service. Arthur Thulin had been a bishop, his wife, Myra, a skilled teacher. Arthur anxiously wrote that he was nearing seventy and might die in Scotland. I replied, "Arthur, you are going to die somewhere; Scotland is a great place to die— but when you die, die with your boots on, not in a comfortable rocking chair." The Thulins went, blessed the lives of many, and Arthur lived several years after their two-year mission.

Many couples have concerns about leaving their homes and families, or being sent to a developing area of the world, or struggling to learn a new language, or trying to keep up with the younger missionaries' tracting and pace of work.

It is not necessary for couples to proselyte in the same way as our young elders and sisters. Couples are often among the most fruitful missionaries because their maturity, seasoned experience, insight, and compassion open many doors in unusual ways.

An example of this comes from a mission president as he describes an unforgettable couple: "I confess," he said, "that when Elder and Sister Leslie arrived, I wondered how well they would do. He was seriously overweight and wore a hearing aid. She was limited with two artificial knee implants. But their spirit was sweet and their enthusiasm so strong. Two wonderfully ordinary people—full of love.

"I felt inspired to send them to Jamestown, Tennessee," he said, "where we had a tiny, struggling branch that had been without missionaries for years. I knew they couldn't tract, and for the first few weeks nothing was noted on their weekly reports. Their letters said, 'We are getting to know the people.'

"After a few weeks their letters told of nonmembers who were attending church with them—at first two, then four, then seven. They had as many as twenty-four investigators at church on one occasion. Soon the baptisms started to flow. No set of missionaries, young or old, equaled the baptisms they brought about."

And the mission president went on to say, "I doubt that either of them could give the missionary discussions in a way that closely resembled the suggested form that we have for the regular missionaries. What they had was a great love for the people. They wove themselves into the fabric of that little community, winning them over with friendship, compassionate service, and understanding hearts.

"Today, the Jamestown Branch is thriving, with a new building and more than 100 members attending. Many contributed their faith and works, but none more significantly or generously than Harry and Frances Leslie."

Compassion . . . service . . . caring—these are qualities of those who truly love their neighbors as themselves.

Though couples such as these have had many years of married life together, they discover new blessings. A husband and wife who serve a mission together will never work so closely and so intensely with one another in such a rewarding effort. Their love will deepen and they will each discover wonderful new dimensions of their companion's inner soul. They will have a greater feeling of unity, and a heavenly relationship will be strengthened.

When Lynn and Dorothea Shawcroft arrived in Ecuador, they were in a state of cultural shock for two weeks and were unable to communicate very well. "We thought, '[Eighteen] months [will be] a very long time,'" they wrote. But then they went on to say, "We saw vividly the conditions in which [some of the] missionaries lived. . . . Our first thoughts were—until we learned more of our own duties—we could at least make life more pleasant for the [full-time missionaries]. So we shopped for pans and ingredients to make cookies and cinnamon rolls. We bought chocolate bars and cut them up to make chocolate chip cookies.

"We learned so much from the [missionaries]. It didn't matter that they learned the language more quickly than we did. Seeing the joy . . . on their faces as they enjoyed a chocolate chip cookie was worth every effort. We represented a bit of home, a bit of something they missed.

"It [may] sound like we did nothing but make cookies for the missionaries. Not so! . . . [We worked] with the [local Church] leaders in activation, teaching, music, . . . genealogy, and welfare. We had open house each week for the . . . missionaries and their investigators. We worked together. . . .

"After teaching a young couple to read or seeing the happiness in a family [because] the father was again attending church, we would walk back to our apartment with a heart that was singing and feet that hardly touched the cobblestone street. Seeing a young mother clap her hands with joy as she truly realized that she was reading, or watching a baby . . .

and knowing that perhaps [this child] wouldn't be alive now had we not [been there at that time]. These experiences, each and every one, made our mission worth every minute of it.

"Was it worth it to struggle with [another] language? It certainly was! . . . Did we feel that we had to keep up with [the younger missionaries]? No. We worked in our own way. . . . Were we accepted? Were we ever!"

Sister Shawcroft recommends that every couple take on their mission a good chocolate chip cookie recipe, lots of love, a good recipe for cinnamon rolls, a strong testimony of the gospel, the scriptures, and then more love.

Each of these couples exemplifies the Savior's teaching to give of ourselves, to reach out to people. In doing so they achieved value to themselves, their families, and to the Church for missionary service rendered in the golden years of their lives.

Deep inside the human soul is a longing to be identified with and involved in something really important. There comes a time in our lives when we are spiritually prepared and ready to be lifted from comfortable and sometimes mundane activities and to make a major decision to respond to a call from our prophet that will ennoble our souls as well as bless others.

The goal of every physically able couple in the Church, just as it is for every nineteen-year-old young man in the Church, should be to serve a mission. No finer example can be given, no finer testimony can be borne by parents to children or grandchildren, than through missionary service in their mature years.

The Savior taught that the first and great commandment is to love the Lord with all our heart, our soul, and our mind. "And the second is like unto it," he said. "Thou shalt love thy neighbour as thyself" (Matthew 22: 37–39). Who are our neighbors? They are *all* of our Father's children. What a blessing we can be to them as we, with mature wisdom and love, bring them the gospel of our Savior, with its eternal covenants and blessings.

We invite bishops to prayerfully review possible calls with appropriate couples, who, after following our Savior's promise to the Nephites to "pray unto the Father in my name; . . . believing that ye shall receive, [and] it shall be given unto you," will know by the Spirit how to respond (3 Nephi 18:19–20).

Great joy and fulfillment will come to them as they humbly serve in their newly expanded world of neighbors.

14

FAMILIES ARE FOREVER

Jesus Christ has committed to mankind the promise that all who believe and are baptized in his holy name and endure in faith to the end will be saved (D&C 20:25). One mission of the Church is to reach and encourage all mankind to hearken unto his voice, for his everlasting covenant is established and is a standard for his people. They are to be messengers and prepare the way before him (D&C 45:2, 9). Inhabitants of the earth are to receive the gospel in order that the kingdom of God might go forth. The Lord has said, "Thou [meaning us] shalt declare glad tidings, yea, publish it upon the mountains, and upon every high place, and among every people that thou shalt be permitted to see. . . . Thou shalt declare repentance and faith on the Savior, and remission of sins by baptism" (D&C 19:29, 31).

Baptism is the gate through which all must enter to accomplish the Lord's desire to bring to pass the immortality and eternal life of man.

One of our family home evening manuals had an inspiring first lesson titled "Families Are Forever." In the lesson, members were instructed to place a number of items on a table, including a marriage certificate, a temple recommend, a picture of a temple, and a baptismal certificate. They were then asked to explain the relationship of these items. Latter-day Saints know that all of these items relate to temple marriage and the possibility of a "forever family." I would like to highlight one of those items on the table—the baptismal certificate.

A "forever family" requires that a couple possess baptismal certificates, be worthy to qualify for temple recommends, and possess a marriage certificate signifying a celestial marriage. Now, what about the millions of our Heavenly Father's children who, if they were baptized, could receive blessings that would lead to becoming an eternal family?

Our full-time missionaries are having increasing success in all parts of the world in bringing souls into the waters of baptism. But their success could be multiplied many times if they had the enthusiastic cooperation of the members of the Church. Many Latter-day Saints seem to have a built-in reluctance to share the gospel with their friends and neighbors. Many of us take pride in referring to the growth of the Church or the success of the worldwide missionary effort but have never fellowshipped an acquaintance or neighbor. When returning mission presidents are asked, "How could you have had more conversions in your mission," we hear the same reply: "If only we could get the members to assist the missionaries by preparing their friends and neighbors to receive them."

Have we forgotten our obligation? Have we forgotten that the Lord said: "Behold, I sent you out to testify and warn the people, and it becometh every man who hath been warned to warn his neighbor. Therefore, they are left without excuse" (D&C 88:81–82).

"I give unto you a commandment, that every man, both elder, priest, teacher, and also member, go to with his might, . . . to prepare and accomplish the things which I have commanded. And let your preaching be the warning voice, every man to his neighbor" (D&C 38:40–41).

Our missionaries are trained to teach the gospel, to teach in an orderly inspired manner, which we hope will lead to baptism. To a missionary, every hour is precious and must be productive. Do you realize that missionaries baptize about one person for every one thousand homes they tract? These same missionaries will baptize six hundred people for every one thousand who are taught in the homes of members—six hundred times more converts when members participate with conviction.

More of these exciting young servants of the Lord are in our wards and branches than ever before. Missionaries are going out better trained, better prepared, with higher hopes and aspirations. Every family that has accepted the gospel is obligated to share it with his neighbor. We can interest people in the gospel by just being natural and sincerely showing our love for them. Emily Dickinson wrote:

> We never know how high we are
> Till we are called to rise
> And then, if we are true to plan
> Our statures touch the skies
>
> (Poem no. 1176)

Those who are reluctant to prepare the way for a teaching opportunity for the missionaries in their neighborhoods are denying themselves rich blessings and are not obeying our prophet's counsel. President Spencer W. Kimball said: "I know this message [every member a missionary] is not new, and we have talked about it before; but I believe the time has come when we must shoulder arms. I think we must change our sights and raise our goals" (Regional Representatives' seminar, 4 Apr. 1974).

The prophet Nephi said: "The day should come that they [that is, we who live in the latter days] must be judged of their works, yea, even the works which were done by the temporal body in their days" (1 Nephi 15:32).

On an airplane flight some time ago, a friend of mine engaged a woman in conversation. He told her about his trip to Anderson, South Carolina, to visit a fourth cousin because he was seeking information concerning some of his ancestors. He asked this woman, "Would you like to know why I am interested in my ancestors who died long ago?"

"Yes, I would," she replied.

"I was trying to find information about my forebears so I could perform certain work for them in the temple. Do you know where the Savior was during the three days his body lay in the tomb following the crucifixion?"

"No. Where?"

"Peter, the apostle, said that Christ preached to the spirits in prison who were disobedient in the days of Noah. Now, do you think the Savior of the world would spend three days preaching to such people if they could not do anything about it?"

"No, I don't. I have never thought of that," she said.

He proceeded to explain baptism for the dead and the resurrection. He quoted Paul: "Else what shall they do which are baptized for the dead, if the dead rise not at all? why are they then baptized for the dead?" (1 Corinthians 15:29). Then he asked, "Do you remember the phrase 'until death do you part' being used when you were married? Your marriage contract ends when either of you dies."

She replied, "I guess that's right, but I had never thought of it that way."

He continued, "My wife died last month, but she is my wife eternally. We were married by one having the priesthood authority to bind in heaven that marriage performed here on earth. We belong to each other eternally, and furthermore, our children belong to us forever."

Just before landing he said to her, "Do you know why we met? It is so that you too can learn about the gospel and be sealed to your husband, your children, and your progenitors for eternity—to become an eternal family."

Soon after this incident, he mailed a copy of Elder LeGrand Richards's book *A Marvelous Work and a Wonder* to the woman and her family and tucked his name card inside. The name of the woman eventually found its way to some full-time missionaries laboring in her city in Pennsylvania. After the missionaries' first contact with her, they wrote, "Mrs. Davis was extremely gracious. You should have seen the light in her eyes when she met us. Brother Cummings had planted a most fertile seed with his testimony and confidence that he and his loved ones would be together after this life. As missionaries we felt at peace. We were impressed that the Lord would attend our efforts because this family was prepared."

Now, do you remember the essentials of a "forever family"? Baptismal certificates, temple recommends, marriage certificate. But first your friends and neighbors must have a baptismal certificate. The conversation of my friend and the woman on the plane planted a desire for that baptismal certificate.

Let us not forget what the Lord has told us: "This is a day of warning, and not a day of many words. For I, the Lord, am not to be mocked in the last days" (D&C 63:58). "And thou shalt declare glad tidings, yea, publish it upon the mountains. . . . And thou shalt do it with all humility, trusting in me" (D&C 19:29–30).

In an effort to stimulate missionary activity, some stakes in Ohio presented a program on the Word of Wisdom entitled "What Makes Mormons Run?" Church leaders encouraged members to bring many friends and neighbors to this meeting. A stake high councilor was sure his neighbors would refuse, and though he felt obligated to invite his next-door neighbors, he kept putting it off, certain they would not accept.

Finally, somewhat embarrassed, he decided not to postpone the challenge any longer. After praying that his approach and words would not be misunderstood by his neighbors, he took the hand of his eight-year-old daughter, and they went next door. There they were warmly greeted and invited in. They extended an invitation to this neighbor family to come and attend the special program. The family agreed to attend.

Now it was much easier for the high councilor to ask other neighbors, friends, associates, even his daughter's piano teacher. His newly found courage led to more success and a comfortable feeling. Over forty people responded to his invitation. He had to charter a bus to transport his guests to the meeting.

And what about the first neighbor he invited? They are now members of the Church, a potential "forever family." Before they were baptized, the high councilor wrote, "I tremble to think that because of my reluctance to share the gospel with my neighbors, this choice family would have lost the blessings of the gospel. Oh, that every Church member could feel this wonderful experience!"

And why did his neighbors decide to investigate the Church? The father of the family said: "If any other neighbor had come to my door to invite me to investigate religion, I would have declined; but we were so impressed with your family, your cleanliness, and your actions. You are always friendly and smiling. Your yard looks so neat and clean, and you are up working in your yard before anyone else is out of bed in the morning. We wanted to learn more about you and your church."

The Lord declared: "All men must repent and be baptized. . . . And by your hands I will work a marvelous work among the children of men, unto the convincing of many of their sins, that they may come unto repentance, and that they may come unto the kingdom of my Father" (D&C 18:42, 44).

If every Latter-day Saint family will become involved—pray as a family for success; select a family to fellowship; set goals and dates for accomplishment; commit themselves to do whatever is appropriate; then fast and pray, and then pray and fast—our warning voice will be heard. This is the day when the harvest is ripe; the press is full. The Lord will bless our efforts, and we will witness friends enter the waters of baptism.

The lives we touch may forget what we said, but they will never forget how we made them feel. Families are forever!

15

TUNING THE STRINGS OF THE NEEDY

Arturo Toscanini, the famous conductor of the New York Philharmonic Orchestra, received a brief, crumpled letter from a lonely sheepherder in the remote mountain area of Wyoming. The man wrote: "Mr. Conductor, I have only two possessions—a radio and an old violin. The batteries in my radio are getting low and will soon die. My violin is so out of tune I can't use it. Please help me. Next Sunday when you begin your concert, sound a loud A so I can tune my A string; then I can tune the other strings. When my radio batteries are dead, I'll have my violin." At the beginning of his next nationwide radio concert from Carnegie Hall, Toscanini announced: "For a dear friend and listener back in the mountains of Wyoming, the orchestra will now sound an A." The musicians all joined together in a perfect A.

The lonely sheepherder needed only one note, just a little help to get back in tune; he could go on from there. He needed someone who cared to assist him with one string; the others would be easy. Then, with all strings in tune—in harmony—the lonely sheepherder would have a source of companionship and joy and could play uplifting strains.

My expressions of encouragement are to God's children whose batteries may be low or whose strings are in need of tuning, those whose souls were once touched by the words and teachings of the Master and his servants but who have been attracted away into other interests and activities. Some may have been neglected or not sufficiently involved in a meaningful Church responsibility; some may have a feeling of injury or hurt or even unworthiness.

Some have allowed themselves to get out of tune. They may have lost the pitch and drifted from the original score. The Savior of the world gave rules to live by and taught principles of love that encompass concern and encouragement. "Come unto me, all ye that labour, and are heavy laden," he said, "and I will give you rest. Take my yoke upon you, and learn of me; for I am meek and lowly in heart: and ye shall find rest unto your souls. For my yoke is easy, and my burden is light" (Matthew 11:28–30).

He did not say "come unto me all you who are perfect," or just the rich, or just the poor, or just the sick, or just the healthy, or just those without sin, or just those who pray the longest. His invitation is to all. His plea to all is to love God, love his children, keep his commandments, and believe that he is the Christ, born of God.

Some who have accepted the teachings of the Savior and have been baptized into his Church are now temporarily lost from the fold—some through their own choosing, but others, many times, by our neglect of them.

Matthew tells of the disciples' last earthly visit with Jesus. They had assembled on the mountain as directed, waiting for their Lord. He was the center of their lives. They worshiped him. Now they knew that he would soon leave them. Where would they go? What would they do? Eleven against the world! What would he tell them?

Then Jesus came and told them: "All power is given unto me in heaven and in earth. Go ye therefore, and teach all nations, baptizing them in the name of the Father, and of the Son, and of the Holy Ghost: Teaching them to observe all things whatsoever I have commanded you: and, lo, I am with you alway, even unto the end of the world" (Matthew 28:18–20).

Those instructions were not only to find and baptize, but to teach. The future of the disciples—as with the Church and its members today—

was now clear. They were to bring new souls unto Christ and to teach them the commandments, the principles of the gospel, love of God and love for one another. They were to teach by the Spirit and with love. None were to be lost, but everyone was to feel the love of the Master through his servants. He knew that to carry the message of the gospel to all nations would require active participation by everyone baptized—not just some, but everyone.

There were strong social barriers among the Jews at that time, yet the Savior mingled freely among the publicans and sinners. They were far different from the Pharisees, who believed sinners should not be guests in their houses. Christ rebuked their unkindliness, saying, "They that be whole need not a physician, but they that are sick" (Matthew 9:12).

Jesus' enemies complained that he mingled and ate with sinners, but he justified his ways and taught more clearly the purpose of God's love toward repentant sinners and the joy in heaven over one sinner who repents. He asked them, "If a man have an hundred sheep, and one of them be gone astray, doth he not leave the ninety and nine, and goeth into the mountains, and seeketh that which is gone astray? And if so be that he find it, verily I say unto you, he rejoiceth more of that sheep, than of the ninety and nine which went not astray. Even so it is not the will of your Father which is in heaven, that one of these little ones should perish" (Matthew 18:12–14).

He concluded: "And when he cometh home, he calleth together his friends and neighbours, saying unto them, Rejoice with me; for I have found my sheep which was lost. I say unto you, that likewise joy shall be in heaven over one sinner that repenteth, more than over ninety and nine just persons, which need no repentance" (Luke 15:6–7).

So it is in the Church today. Michael Duffy tells of his experience:

"I didn't catch their names or pay much attention to what they were saying, except they were from the Mormon church. Somehow they had found out I was a Mormon and asked if I wanted home teachers. I hadn't been to Church for sixteen years! I don't know exactly why I said yes. It seemed that many events had fallen into place to convince me that there was a missing link in my life. Previously, we had lived next door to a

107

Mormon family. We did not go to church, but I was reminded that our two sons had never been blessed and had never attended church. My wife was not a Mormon, nor even a Christian. Yet she agreed that something was missing.

"Home teachers soon contacted us and began regular visits. This started a process that would take many months, and change my family forever. I began attending priesthood meeting—infrequently at first, then regularly. I was finally able to overcome my Word of Wisdom problem. Our oldest son, now five, started attending Sunday School. We even began paying a little tithing. My wife supported me, but was not interested in the Church. Then one day two missionaries knocked at our door. After many months, having just been ordained an elder, I baptized and confirmed my wife a member of the Church. We were later sealed as a family in the Washington Temple.

"As I look back on the many circumstances that took place, I fondly remember the love, prayers, and fellowship of the bishopric, elders quorum presidency, and others. We were truly blessed that we lived in a ward that actively worked with less-active members, that the elders quorum president (the position I now hold) placed special emphasis on reactivation, and that even a member of the stake presidency took a personal interest in us."

A few years ago I drove to the Los Angeles Airport with a busy radio executive and learned that he and his wife, though born in the Church, had never participated. Their social life of parties and weekends for fun and escape dominated their lives. After eight years of marriage and three children, they were becoming concerned about their lifestyle, but they had done nothing about it.

Different sets of home teachers came and went. Then a new home teacher—a true shepherd—came into their lives, and after a time he got this man to commit to go to church once. The man said that he would not give up smoking and drinking; he had made a firm resolve not to live the Word of Wisdom, and if he was not welcome in church because of it, so be it. The home teacher replied, "You are welcome, and I will pick you up."

The first Sunday when the man attended church, he waited for someone to move away from him because of the strong tobacco odor, but that didn't happen. "They will ask me to pray or work in the Church," he said to himself. That didn't happen either.

The home teacher did not phone on Sunday mornings to give him a chance to make an excuse and back out; rather, he drove to the home and asked, "Are you ready?" He picked the man up every Sunday for over a year.

Then the couple began reading Elder LeGrand Richards's *A Marvelous Work and a Wonder* and learned that the Church consisted of much more than just the Word of Wisdom. They soon learned it is a church of love, not a church of fear. They learned of the mission of the Savior and of our Heavenly Father and of repentance. They became so proud of the Church they had been born into that the Word of Wisdom no longer was an important issue. The man didn't go through the pangs of quitting smoking. It just happened. There were so many other principles of the gospel that now were so important in his life. He told me, "I found myself working on our new chapel and then one day quietly telling the bishop, 'I'm ready now. You can call on me to pray.'"

The Savior taught Peter, "When thou art converted, strengthen thy brethren" (Luke 22:32). Souls are committed to the care of the Church; we are to watch over and keep them in the right way, to remember their names and nourish them.

An older couple living in a little Mormon community in Idaho had been members of the Church all their lives. The husband was eighty-six years old and his wife eighty-four. He was still a priest in the Aaronic Priesthood. New home teachers who had heard about this family's lack of interest in the Church asked if they could go to their home. The couple were pleased that someone cared about them. The home teachers taught them the principles of the gospel, and they responded. The man became an elder and with his wife, earned the privilege of going to the temple and being married for time and eternity.

If thoughtful home teachers had not visited them, this couple would probably have died without having received essential blessings of the gospel. Caring shepherds might have been able to reach them years before, when the family was growing up. They were grateful that home teachers finally had the courage to come.

People who drift away from the true doctrines usually know in their hearts something is missing. The kernel of truth, though small, remains, never to be replaced with fame or money or worldly pleasures.

The Savior placed a little child in the midst of the disciples and taught that they must become as little children in order to enter into the kingdom of heaven. He said, "The Son of man is come to save that which was lost" (Matthew 18:11).

Michael Weir tells his story:

"My marriage had failed. I was living a life contrary to the principles of the Church. Not only was I not active but I had also lost confidence in my ability to go back. I became successful in business, drove the nicest car, and bought expensive clothes. I had everything that the world could want.

"One day, my company hired Ken Wheeler, whom I knew to be a Mormon by the way he acted. We became friends, and he invited me to church. I wanted to go but didn't feel worthy. He continued to invite me, and I continued to refuse. I wanted to get back, but I didn't have the strength to do it. One night, alone in my apartment, I became very depressed and broke into uncontrollable sobs. I prayed to the Lord and begged for his help. The next day Ken asked me how I was doing; he could sense something was wrong. Putting his arms around me, he said, 'The Lord still loves you, and we do, too. Why don't you come back home?' That was the answer to my prayers; that was the help I had begged for the night before.

"I came home. I felt uncomfortable at first, but the feeling that everyone cared made it easier. Today, I don't drive the nicest car or wear the fanciest clothes, but I feel richer than ever." He concluded, "Those who have fallen away want so badly to come back, but they are afraid to make the move. They don't lose their testimony; they lose confidence in themselves."

Those who stray need friends—friends who know the Shepherd.

Seldom do people cease coming to church because of doctrine; they are waiting for a show of genuine love and friendly fellowship to heal their hurts or doubts.

Nephi tells us that "the Lord God worketh not in darkness. He doeth not anything save it be for the benefit of the world; for he loveth the world, even that he layeth down his own life that he may draw all men unto him. . . . He saith: Come unto me all ye ends of the earth. . . . Hath he commanded any that they should not partake of his salvation? . . . Nay; but . . . hath given it free for all men; and . . . hath commanded his people that they should persuade all men to repentance" (2 Nephi 26:23–25, 27).

We are God's children, and he expects us to find, teach, and recover those whose strings may need tuning. May we be directed by the pure love of Christ to sound for them the perfect note of A.

16

BRINGING THE SHEEP BACK TO THE FOLD

In chapter 15 of Luke, we find three parables of the Savior that impress upon his followers the importance and urgency of searching for that which is lost.

The first parable talks about the lost sheep: "What man of you, having an hundred sheep, if he lose one of them, doth not leave the ninety and nine in the wilderness, and go after that which is lost, until he find it? And when he hath found it, he layeth it on his shoulders, rejoicing." Jesus then declares: "I say unto you, that likewise joy shall be in heaven over one sinner that repenteth, more than over ninety and nine just persons, which need no repentance" (Luke 15:4–7).

In the second parable, Jesus talks about the lost coin: "What woman having ten pieces of silver, if she lose one piece, doth not light a candle, and sweep the house, and seek diligently till she find it? And when she hath found it, she calleth her friends and her neighbours together, saying, Rejoice with me; for I have found the piece which I had lost." The Savior concludes, "Likewise, I say unto you, there is joy in the presence of the angels of God over one sinner that repenteth" (Luke 15:8–10).

The third parable tells the story of the prodigal son, who asked his father for his "portion of goods" and then went to a far country and lost his inheritance through riotous living. When famine came and he found that he could not survive, he determined to return to his father to beg forgiveness and ask to be made a hired servant. As he approached, his father saw him coming, had compassion on him, and ordered his servants, "Bring forth the best robe, and put it on him; and put a ring on his hand, and shoes on his feet: and bring hither the fatted calf, and kill it; and let us eat, and be merry: for this my son was dead, and is alive again; he was lost, and is found. And they began to be merry" (Luke 15:11–24).

The gospel teaches us that every member of the Church has an obligation to strengthen his fellow members. The Savior himself instructed the apostle Peter: "I have prayed for thee, that thy faith fail not: and when thou art converted, strengthen thy brethren" (Luke 22:32).

There is an unusual concern being expressed by the First Presidency and the Quorum of the Twelve Apostles over the increasing numbers of Latter-day Saints who are listed on quorum and ward reports as less-active.

We remind you that

Every less-active man has a bishop, quorum president, and home teachers.

Every less-active woman has a bishop, Relief Society president, and visiting teachers.

Every less-active young woman has a bishop and a Young Women's president.

Every less-active young man has a bishop and quorum president.

And every member of the Church has a stake president or a mission president.

President Harold B. Lee taught: "There is no new organization necessary to take care of the needs of this people. All that is necessary is to put the priesthood of God to work" (in Conference Report, Oct. 1972, 124). Our attention to this alarming trend of inactivity must now become one of our most urgent priorities. The worth of all souls is great in the sight of God, whether they be nonmembers, less-active members, or active members.

The Prophet Joseph Smith referred to this obligation in a letter to the Saints written while he was imprisoned in Liberty Jail in Missouri in March 1839: "Thy mind, O man! if thou wilt lead a soul unto salvation, must stretch as high as the utmost heavens, and search into and contemplate the darkest abyss, and the broad expanse of eternity—thou must commune with God. How much more dignified and noble are the thoughts of God, than the vain imaginations of the human heart! None but fools will trifle with the souls of men!" (*History of The Church of Jesus Christ of Latter-day Saints,* ed. B. H. Roberts, 2d ed. rev., 7 vols. [Salt Lake City: The Church of Jesus Christ of Latter-day Saints, 1932–51], 3:295).

If we truly love the Lord, we will feed his sheep (see John 21:15–17). How will we do that? Through love and eternal friendship, not force or pressure.

A few years ago I heard about a farsighted home teacher in an elders quorum who was given the name of a less-active member. On his way to priesthood meeting early one Sunday morning, he called at the home of this member.

"I'm on my way to priesthood meeting and thought you might like a ride," he explained.

The man, startled and somewhat angry at this interruption of his Sunday rest, said, "No, I'm not interested," and slammed the door.

The following Sunday morning the home teacher again rang the man's doorbell. "Just dropped by in case you've changed your mind," he told the startled man. "We'd really like you to join us."

"Go away! Leave me alone!" the man shouted, slamming the door.

A week later the home teacher rang the doorbell again. This time he added, "We have a great group of men. We need you. You're a member of our quorum. Would you mind if I stopped by next Sunday?" The man decided that the only way to stop his early-morning caller was to go to priesthood meeting and prove he was not interested, so he finally agreed.

The next Sunday, when the home teacher rang the doorbell, the man was dressed and ready to prove his lack of interest. But the spirit of the priesthood meeting, the friendly handclasps, and the sincere interest of the quorum members changed the attitude and awakened the conscience of a man who needed a gentle push. He soon became an active member of the quorum.

There are tens of thousands of good people who have quietly drifted away and are now waiting for a knock on their door. Those who have strayed must experience a doctrinal conversion and social integration by someone who cares.

Loren Eiseley tells about walking along a stormy beach late one afternoon "with the wind roaring at his back and the seagulls screaming" overhead. Tourists who came to the beach would collect shellfish and sea life tossed up each night, boil them in large kettles, and take the shells home as souvenirs. Eiseley walked far down the beach around a point away from the collectors and saw "a gigantic rainbow of incredible perfection." Toward its foot he "discerned a human figure . . . gazing . . . at something in the sand. . . . A starfish had thrust its arms up stiffly and was holding its body away from the stifling mud."

"Is it still alive?" Eiseley asked.

"'Yes,' [said the man standing in the rainbow] and with a quick . . . gentle movement he picked up the star and spun it far out into the sea. 'It may live,' he said, 'if the offshore pull is strong enough.'"

At first Eiseley felt only the futility of the man's efforts, "throwing one starfish at a time back into the sea when it nightly tosses out hundreds." He walked away, looking sadly "at the shell collectors . . . [and] the steaming kettles in which . . . voiceless things were being boiled alive."

The next morning Eiseley again went to the beach. Again the star thrower was there. "Silently [Eiseley] . . . picked up a still-living star, spinning it far out into the waves. . . . 'I understand,' [he] said. 'Call me [a star] thrower [also].'"

Of throwing the starfish back he wrote, "It was like sowing—the sowing of life on an infinitely gigantic scale." He saw the star thrower stoop and throw once more. Eiseley joined with him. They "flung and flung again while all about [them] roared the insatiable waters." They "alone and small in that immensity, hurled back the living stars." They set their shoulders and "cast, . . . slowly, deliberately, and well. The task was not to be assumed lightly" (Loren Eiseley, *The Star Thrower* [New York: Harcourt, Brace, Jovanovich, 1978], 171–73, 184). Each moment counted if they were to rescue the starfish that they sought to save.

We need star throwers—throwers who have vision, who have a sense of discipleship with the Savior, who feel the need to save where there is still life and hope and value and who will not to let that life die on a friendless beach but will hurl it back to where it belongs. Then we may better understand our Lord's commandment: "Thou shalt love thy neighbour as thyself" (Matthew 19:19).

The heart and soul of activating our neighbors who have become less active in the Church is found in these four keys:

1. Fellowshipping them with genuine love and concern.

2. Teaching them the gospel in their homes.

3. Involving them in temple preparation seminars.

4. Involving them in Church assignments and callings as quickly as possible.

Love is the basic ingredient and motive for successful activation. One less-active woman was touched when her home teacher told her, "We have a place set for you at our table, and it won't be the same without you." In addition to his words, of course, he showed a genuine feeling of love and concern. She accepted his dinner invitation—and eventually returned to Church activity.

An enterprising and perceptive bishop in California set a goal for his ward to reactivate every less-active person in his ward. He told his ward members, "If you care enough, you'll find a way to reach them." He reserved one night a week to visit less-active members and tried to visit two or three families that night.

On his first visit to a family, he would talk about non-Church topics—fishing, the children, school activities, or other subjects the family members were interested in. "They needed to know that we care," he said. "The next time I visited, we'd talk about the Church. I don't do home teaching—I do fellowshipping."

How did he get them active? After finding out what their interests were, he would put them to work. As soon as appropriate, they were called to positions where they could serve without fear of responsibilities beyond their present abilities.

He concluded: "At all of our ward committee meetings, we report on less-active members before anything else. That gets everyone involved. If someone starts to talk about something else, I interrupt; I want to know about the less-actives first of all. We don't do anything extraordinary; we just follow the program and let people know we care. You'll find ways to get them active, if you love them."

One stake in southern California started a reactivation program in which the bishopric of each ward appointed effective teams from the high priests and elders quorums to work with less-active members. As these special teaching teams visited each family, they stated at the offset that they had been sent by the bishop. They then asked if they might come once or twice each week to teach the family the gospel. Gospel messages were adapted to the needs of the family members.

In six months fifty-nine individuals were activated in this stake, mostly as a direct result of teaching in the home by hand-picked, capable teachers. The stake president attributed his stake's success to (a) the bishops' being asked by constituted authority to recover those who were less-active, (b) careful selection of the most capable teachers, and (c) the diligence and love of the teachers.

An elders quorum in Colorado reported wonderful success in reactivating members through effective home teaching and the use of filmstrips. Seven quorum members each purchased film projectors for use in the program. One prospective elder had remarked, "Please don't send the home teachers to my home anymore." Then he and his wife were visiting at the home of another less-active member when the home teachers arrived with their film projector. He saw the filmstrip, his heart was touched, and he invited the home teacher to return to his home.

The quorum formed committees, athletic as well as social, to plan activities to prove to less-active members that there is fun and joy in the Church. Members of the quorum held an overnight campout in the mountains, where they sat around a campfire for six hours discussing gospel principles. "We had a real spiritual feast," the quorum president reported.

To keep each former less-active quorum member committed to the Church, the quorum president works with the bishop in preparing the person for a calling and developing an appropriate position for him. This quorum has caught the spirit exemplified by the Lord: "And as all have not faith, seek ye diligently and teach one another" (D&C 88:118).

When one less-active brother was approached by his priesthood leaders, he told them, "I'm not inactive; it's just that you don't need me." Men, women, and youth will respond to our invitations to participate when they feel they are needed. There is an appropriate calling for everyone.

Some time ago a man told me how he became lost in the middle of a ward with five hundred members. "My wife and I had our first contact with the Church when two sweet, spiritual missionaries called. They came, they taught, they converted. We literally lived off their spirit. Then, as many converts know, those two wonderful elders were transferred.

"It was extremely difficult for us to keep that same spirit," he said. "We felt we could not go it alone. We withdrew from Church activity. My wife told the visiting teachers not to come back, and we asked the home teachers to leave us alone. I suppose in the elders quorum they discussed some 'lost' brethren who needed to be 'found.' Yes, I was lost. One day there came a knock at our front door. As I opened it, I saw a young, smiling, freckle-faced man who said he was the elders quorum president. He asked if he could talk to me for a few minutes.

"In the coming weeks he came many times to bring us vegetables from his garden, eggs from his chickens, a birthday card for our daughter. Sometimes he came just to talk. He got me involved in the ward sports program. He even apologized for anyone who may have hurt our feelings. What did he do that got us back? He loved us. He was sincere. He cared. He shared with me his personal testimony. He helped me to search my soul. He helped me to pray to my Father in heaven.

"For the love this man gave my family, we will be eternally grateful. The Lord has poured out his blessings on us. We have been to the temple and have been sealed for eternity. We have returned to the temple many times and gained further light and knowledge promised to us.

"I am now working with this elders quorum president as his counselor. My wife is teaching Primary and is a visiting teacher. I was lost, but because someone cared, because someone took time, because someone took the risk of showing his love and concern, I was found and was able to lead my family back to the Lord. I plead with all members of the Church to look around and help guide lost children back to their Heavenly Father."

In a survey of less-active and reactivated members, we learned the following:

1. The three most commonly mentioned reasons for inactivity center on feelings of not feeling needed or accepted in the ward. Only about one-fourth of those who become less active say their decision to do so was a conscious decision based on their unwillingness to follow the teachings of the Church.

2. From one-third to one-half of those returning to activity say they did so because of a desire to have more religion in their lives.

3. As many as one-fourth of those returning to activity did so because someone invited them.

4. The first four to eight years are the most crucial years in keeping new converts from becoming less active.

5. The teenage years are the most crucial years in helping members remain active.

6. Members who become less active are more likely to return to activity if they are encouraged to do so within the first few years after their inactivity began.

Recently a stake presidency decided to put an activation plan to a test and to personally visit some prospective elders. They reported: "The first brother we visited was a less-active elder. He wept and thanked us for coming. Since our visit, he has accepted a calling in the Church. The second, a prospective elder, also wept. He promised to give up his cigarettes and to prepare for Melchizedek Priesthood ordination at our next stake conference. The third, also a prospective elder, was pleased to have us visit. A counselor in the stake presidency developed a marvelous rapport with him and is working with his family in addition to the special home teachers assigned. And the fourth visit was to a prospective elder who warmly received us, reaffirmed his less-active lifestyle, but agreed to receive some materials about temple marriage."

The stake presidency then added, "Not bad for just two weeks of visiting!" They have a new appreciation of how successfully we can reach those who are less active.

In wards that have made great strides in their activation efforts, members have a legitimate sense of their importance, genuine pride in their callings, and respect and admiration for their leaders. Bishops have an instinctive warmth, cordiality, and sense of genuine interest in the lives and welfare of every member. We must continue to develop and cultivate this positive love and concern for each member, looking beyond ourselves and reaching out to grasp the hands of those who have wandered away and lead them back to the fold.

Let me summarize the guiding principles of the activation program:

First, priesthood and auxiliary leaders must be determined to set the activation guidelines in motion.

Second, they must have faith that the activation of men and women and families is possible.

Third, the individual or family must be taught the gospel, either in their homes or by attending a temple preparation seminar so that they might become converted.

Fourth, and most importantly, leaders need to qualify themselves to obtain the companionship of the Holy Ghost to assist them in touching the lives of the less-active members.

President Spencer W. Kimball said of our responsibility to strengthen less-active members: "I am very hopeful that the Church will stay with the emphasis on these challenges for several years, so that we can truly make a significant difference. It doesn't mean that other things must go undone during this time, but we need to concentrate on the things that are most critical. There are so many marvelous benefits that await us as a people if we succeed, and I am positive we will succeed. So much depends upon our willingness to make up our minds, collectively and individually, that present levels of performance are not acceptable, either to ourselves or to the Lord. In saying that, I am not calling for flashy, temporary differences in our performance levels, but a quiet resolve to do a better job" (*Lengthening Our Stride*, Regional Representatives' seminar, 3 Oct. 1974).

We can change the present flow of men and women and boys and girls into the dark pool of inactivity. May each of us reach out to our brothers and sisters in the gospel and help bring them back to the fold.

WHATSOEVER IS LIGHT, IS GOOD

ALMA 32:35

17

OUR DUTY IS TO LOVE EVERYONE

As members of The Church of Jesus Christ of Latter-day Saints, we testify of Christ. Our hope is in Christ. Our salvation is in Christ. Our efforts, hopes, and desires to build up the kingdom of God on earth are centered in and through his holy name. We proclaim, as did John the Baptist upon seeing Jesus approaching the river Jordan, "Behold the Lamb of God, which taketh away the sin of the world" (John 1:29). He taught the doctrines of his gospel, so that every soul may have the opportunity to gain the blessings of eternal life.

As we strive to fulfill our divine responsibility to spread his gospel, we need the full measure of every promised blessing for his people: belief, patience, obedience, charity, wisdom, and faith in his word and a testimony of it.

I believe that our Father planted into our souls a special ingredient that, if used, will influence us toward heavenly things. Families or individuals wondering how to better share the gospel or to show deeper concern for new members, or missionaries wanting to touch the hearts of those they are teaching, have available to them this heavenly influence. It may bring to us our greatest joy. It can help us overcome fear, peer pressure, hatred, selfishness, evil, and even sin.

This special ingredient, which is powerful beyond words, was explained by the Savior himself when he was asked which was the great commandment of the law. He said: "Thou shalt love the Lord thy God with all thy heart, and with all thy soul, and with all thy mind. This is the first and great commandment. And the second is like unto it, Thou shalt love thy neighbour as thyself. On these two commandments hang all the law and the prophets" (Matthew 22:37–40).

Love is this divine ingredient. It alone describes what can be our perfect relationship to our Heavenly Father and our family and neighbors, and the means by which we accomplish his work.

The two commandments—to love God and to love man—had been taught separately by Jewish teachers, but Jesus brought them together and made the second like the first. By the example of his own life, he made love of God and love of mankind the heart of the gospel. "By this," he said, "shall all men know that ye are my disciples, if ye have love one to another" (John 13:35).

Besides loving God, we are commanded to follow what to many is a more difficult commandment: to love all, even enemies, and to go beyond the barriers of race or class or family relationships. It is easy, of course, to be kind to those who are kind to us—the usual standard of friendly reciprocity. But we are commanded to cultivate genuine fellowship and even a kinship with every human being on earth. Whom should we bar from our circle? We might deny ourselves a nearness to our Savior because of our prejudices of neighborhood or possession or race—attitudes that Christ would surely condemn. Love has no boundary, no limitation of good will.

To the lawyer who asked, "Who is my neighbour?" the Savior gave a parable that is the pure essence of love:

"A certain man went down from Jerusalem to Jericho, and fell among thieves, which stripped him of his raiment, and wounded him, and departed, leaving him half dead.

"And by chance there came down a certain priest that way: and when he saw him, he passed by on the other side.

"And likewise a Levite, when he was at the place, came and looked on him, and passed him by on the other side.

"But a certain Samaritan, as he journeyed, came where he was: and when he saw him, he had compassion on him,

"And went to him, and bound up his wounds, pouring in oil and wine, and set him on his own beast, and brought him to an inn, and took care of him,

"And on the morrow when he departed, he took out two pence, and gave them to the host, and said unto him, Take care of him; and whatsoever thou spendest more, when I come again, I will repay thee.

"Which now of these three, thinkest thou, was neighbour unto him that fell among the thieves?

"And he said, He that shewed mercy on him. Then said Jesus unto him, Go, and do thou likewise" (Luke 10:30–37).

The essential difference between the Samaritan and the other two men was that one had a compassionate heart and the others had selfish hearts. Though the Jews looked down upon Samaritans, the priest and the Levite—both of whom were Jews—should have come to the aid of the unfortunate man but did not.

Elder John A. Widtsoe wrote:

"The full and essential nature of love we may not understand, but there are tests by which it may be recognized.

"Love is always founded in truth. . . . Lies and deceit, or any other violation of the moral law, are proofs of love's absence. Love perishes in the midst of untruth. . . . Thus, . . . he who falsifies to his loved one, or offers her any act contrary to truth, does not really love her.

"Further, love does not offend or hurt or injure the loved one. . . . Cruelty is as absent from love . . . as truth is from untruth. . . .

"Love is a positive, active force. It helps the loved one. If there is need, love tries to supply it. If there is weakness, love supplants it with strength. . . . Love that does not help is a faked or transient love.

"Good as these tests are, there is a greater one. True love sacrifices for the loved one. . . . That is the final test. Christ gave of Himself, gave his life, for us, and thereby proclaimed the reality of his love for his mortal brethren and sisters" (*An Understandable Religion* [Salt Lake City: Deseret Book, 1944], 22).

Knowing that we should love is not enough. But when knowledge is applied through service, love can secure for us the blessings of heaven. Jesus taught: "Greater love hath no man than this, that a man lay down his life for his friends" (John 15:13).

A commercial airplane plunged into the Potomac River near Washington, D. C., some years ago, and an unidentified passenger gave his life for his "unknown friends." Bystanders watched in amazement as he caught the life preserver lowered from the helicopter to rescue those in the water. Rather than save himself, he passed the life preserver over to another person. The helicopter returned, and he again passed the life preserver to another. "Why doesn't he hold on and save himself?" someone shouted. After others near him were saved, people on the shore watched in anguish as he slowly sank and disappeared into the frozen waters.

"If a single man achieves the highest kind of love," wrote Mahatma Gandhi, "it will be sufficient to neutralize the hate of millions."

God does not love us because we are lovable, have a pleasing personality or a good sense of humor, or at rare times show exceptional kindness. In spite of who we are and what we have done, God wants to pour out his love on us, for the unlovable are also precious unto him. "A man filled with the love of God," wrote the Prophet Joseph Smith, "is not content with blessing his family alone, but ranges through the whole world, anxious to bless the whole human race" (*History of The Church of Jesus Christ of Latter-day Saints,* ed. B. H. Roberts, 2d ed. rev., 7 vols. [Salt Lake City: The Church of Jesus Christ of Latter-day Saints, 1932–1951], 4:227).

How can we earn God's love? The Savior taught: "If ye keep my commandments, ye shall abide in my love; even as I have kept my Father's commandments, and abide in his love" (John 15:10).

Love is a gift of God, and as we obey his laws and genuinely learn to serve others, we develop his love in our lives.

Love of God is the means of unlocking divine powers that help us to live worthily and to overcome the world. The Savior rejected worldly methods of promoting great causes. Money to buy influence—he had none. Publications—he never used. The sword was contrary to his purposes. The people of his own nation disowned him. He planted his ideals in the hearts of only a few, who met, listened, prayed, and believed in his words. As taught by the Master, they went among other men and, through act and word, passed on the new ideals—by love unfeigned and by friendship, not by force—and so the work spread.

God accomplishes his purposes heart to heart. The prophet Nephi helps us to understand this. He said: "It is the love of God, which sheddeth itself abroad in the hearts of the children of men; wherefore, it is the most desirable above all things" (1 Nephi 11:22). The depth and magnitude of God's love for all his children is emphasized in the writings of John: "God so loved the world, that he gave his only begotten Son, that whosoever believeth in him should not perish, but have everlasting life" (John 3:16).

Brother and Sister Willes Cheney were called as missionaries to the Canada Halifax Mission and assigned to Cranbrook, Newfoundland. The instructions from their mission president were: "Go up there and strengthen the branch. Find some housing so the people will have their own place to meet in. And be ambassadors of good will." This faithful couple touched many lives. Brother Cheney reported of their numerous successes with people and concluded with this tribute to his lovely companion: "Aside from the many examples, the major contribution to our success was Sister Cheney. Her whole mission was a labor of love—teaching how to plant a garden, can, sew, quilt, and give compassionate service. She was loved by all because of her excellent example as a wife, as a mother, and as a friend." He concluded, "We helped the branch acquire a chapel and saw twenty-seven new members come into the Church, and many who were less active return." This lovely couple had demonstrated their love of the Lord and for their newfound neighbors, though they were far away from home.

Someone has written, "Love is a verb." It requires doing, not just saying or thinking. The test is in what we do, how we act, for love is conveyed in word or deed.

John the Beloved, who had a special closeness to our Lord, wrote:

"Herein is love, not that we loved God, but that he loved us, and sent his Son to be the propitiation for our sins. Beloved, if God so loved us, we ought also to love one another" (1 John 4:10–11).

Through paying the debt of sin for each of us, Jesus brings us, if we desire, to his Father. We sing these expressive words, which truly convey our feelings:

> I stand all amazed at the love Jesus offers me,
> Confused at the grace that so fully he proffers me.
> I tremble to know that for me he was crucified,
> That for me, a sinner, he suffered, he bled and died.
>
> I marvel that he would descend from his throne divine
> To rescue a soul so rebellious and proud as mine,
> That he should extend his great love unto such as I,
> Sufficient to own, to redeem, and to justify.
>
> I think of his hands pierced and bleeding to pay the debt!
> Such mercy, such love, and devotion can I forget?
> No, no, I will praise and adore at the mercy seat,
> Until at the glorified throne I kneel at his feet.
>
> (*Hymns,* no. 193)

May each of us strive always to be obedient to all the laws and ordinances of the gospel, strengthened by our compliance with the great commandments to love God and our neighbors.

18

BUILDING AND
STRENGTHENING
MARRIAGE

Today we are witnessing an unending assault on the traditional family. Sacred values of human goodness, discipline, and love and honor for God our Eternal Father are being challenged as never before. A new self-centered generation is making the family a prime target of continuing belittlement. Marriage is being downgraded or shunned, parenthood degraded and avoided. These, with other disturbing influences, are resulting in a torrent of evil temptations for instant gratification and the demeaning of marriage and the sacred roles of wife and mother.

We learn from the scriptures that the divine intent is that marriage be an eternal union with family relationships enduring throughout eternity. After the earth was created, God made man in his own image and gave him dominion over the earth. By the side of man stood the woman, sharing with him the divinely bestowed honor and dignity of supremacy over all other creations. God said, "It is not good that the man should be alone; I will make him an help meet for him" (Genesis 2:18).

The Lord also instructed, "Therefore shall a man leave his father and his mother, and shall cleave unto his wife: and they shall be one flesh" (Genesis 2:24), thereby giving sanction to the union of male and female in authorized marriage, which is heaven-planned for the creation of mortal bodies.

The earliest recorded commandment to Adam and Eve was to "be fruitful, and multiply, and replenish the earth" (Genesis 1:28). We regard children as gifts from God, committed to our care for loving, nurturing, and careful training. The Lord instructed us to "teach [our] children to pray, and to walk uprightly before the Lord" (D&C 68:28). They are not to be mistreated or abused; rather, they are part of a family with the potential of eternal relationship.

President Spencer W. Kimball explained: "The Lord organized the whole program in the beginning with a father who procreates, provides, and loves and directs, and a mother who conceives and bears and nurtures and feeds and trains. The Lord could have organized it otherwise but chose to have a unit with responsibility and purposeful associations where children train and discipline each other and come to love, honor, and appreciate each other. The family is the great plan of life as conceived and organized by our Father in heaven" ("The Family Influence," *Ensign,* July 1973, 15).

Marriage was meant to be and can be a loving, binding, and harmonious relationship between a husband and wife.

As we contemplate our Lord's declaration to Moses, "This is my work and my glory—to bring to pass the immortality and eternal life of man" (Moses 1:39), we reflect with sadness upon the present serious trend of families and homes being torn apart through divorce. A major underlying cause of divorce seems to be in not understanding that marriage and families are God-given and God-ordained. If people understood the full meaning, there would be less divorce and its attendant unhappiness. Couples would plan for a happy marriage relationship based on divine instruction. If couples understood from the beginning of their romance that their marriage relationship could be blessed with promises and conditions extending into the eternities, divorce would not even be a considered alternative when difficulties arise. The current philosophy—

get a divorce if it doesn't work out—handicaps a marriage from the beginning.

The ever-increasing rise in divorce is ample evidence of how acceptable divorce has become as the popular solution to unhappy or "not-quite-up-to-expectation" marriages. But no matter how acceptable divorce has become—how quick and easy to obtain—it is tragic and painful, not only at the outset, but also in the years to come. Divorce can never really be final. How can mothers and fathers divorce themselves from their own flesh and blood children, or from the memories of days and years of shared experiences that have become part of their very lives?

Divorce rarely occurs without immense emotional, social, and financial upheaval. Most people underestimate the alienation, bitterness, disruption, and frustration between a divorcing couple and among their children, friends, and relatives. Some never adjust to the resulting emotional consequences.

Perhaps most tragic of all is that more than 60 percent of all divorces involve children under eighteen years of age. Children of divorce all too often have a higher delinquency rate and less self-confidence than do children in homes where parents are happily married, and they tend to be more promiscuous and more likely to have unhappy marriages themselves.

Considering the enormous importance of marriage, it is rather astonishing that we don't make better preparation for its success. Usually, young couples date for a few months or for a year or two, enjoying romance and getting acquainted. But once they are married, they soon learn that romance must blend with spiritual beliefs, in-law relationships, money issues, and serious discussions involving ethics, children, and the running of a home. Too many people are inadequately prepared for this lofty responsibility. They go to college for years to prepare for a vocation or a profession that is not nearly so rewarding or important as a good marriage. Serious transgressions, as well as injured lives, all too frequently make it clear that husband-and-wife relationships deserve a great deal more prayerful attention than many are giving them. Fewer marriages would become troubled, and more would be happier, if couples visited a warm-hearted bishop or counselor who could suggest ways to avoid pitfalls, and who could encourage them to thoughtfully use self-discipline and needed restraint and develop the loving attribute of unselfishness.

President Harold B. Lee once received this letter from a married woman: "When we thought that the end was here and that there was only one thing to do and that was to get a divorce, we had been told that we should counsel with our bishop. At first . . . we hesitated, because he was just a young man. . . . But he was our bishop so we went to see him. We poured out our souls to our young bishop. He sat and listened silently, and when we ran out of conversation he said simply, 'Well, my wife and I, we had problems, too, and we learned how to solve them.' That is all . . . he said. But you know there was something that happened as a result of that young bishop's statement. We walked out of there and we said, 'Well, if they can solve their problems, what is the matter with us?'" ("General Priesthood Address," *Ensign,* Jan. 1974, 100).

Our concern is that many married couples don't take their marriages seriously enough to work at them, protect them, nurture them, cultivate them day in and day out, week in and week out, yearlong, quarter-century long, half-a-century long, forever.

Middle-age divorce is particularly distressing; it indicates that mature people, the backbone of our society, are not working carefully enough to preserve their marriages. Divorces granted to people over forty-five have increased at an alarming rate. A couple who consider breaking up their marriage—a couple who may have reared their children, who possibly have grandchildren—and decide to go their separate ways, need to realize that every divorce is the result of selfishness on the part of one party or both.

In Malachi we read: "The Lord hath been witness between thee and the wife of thy youth, against whom thou hast dealt treacherously: yet is she thy companion, and the wife of thy covenant. . . . Therefore take heed to your spirit, and let none deal treacherously against the wife of his youth" (Malachi 2:14–15).

Marriage is a covenant. Two of the Ten Commandments deal directly with preserving the sanctity of marriage: "Thou shalt not commit adultery" and "Thou shalt not covet thy neighbour's wife" (Exodus 20:14, 17).

Jesus magnified the law against adultery: "But I say unto you, that whosoever looketh on a woman to lust after her hath committed adultery with her already in his heart" (Matthew 5:28).

Successful marriage comes as a result of the faithfulness of a man and a woman to each other, a faithfulness that began when each chose the other. It is a privilege indeed for a couple to live harmoniously with their chosen mate and to continue acquiring a depth of love, oneness, and wisdom that can be shared with each other now and throughout all eternity.

Marriage is sustained by faith and knowledge of its divine establishment and by the energy of love. A wise man explained, "When the satisfaction or the security of another person becomes as significant to one as one's own satisfaction and security, then the state of love exists" (Harry Stack Sullivan).

A strong, shared conviction that there is something eternally precious about the marriage relationship builds faith to resist evil. Marriage should be beautiful and fulfilling, with joy beyond our fondest dreams, for "neither is the man without the woman, neither the woman without the man, in the Lord" (1 Corinthians 11:11).

Latter-day Saints need not divorce—there are solutions to marriage problems. If, as husband and wife, you are having serious misunderstandings, or if you feel some strain or tension building up in your marriage, you should humbly get on your knees together and ask God our Father, with a sincere heart and real intent, to lift the darkness that is over your relationship so that you may receive the needed light, see your errors, repent of your wrongs, forgive each other, and receive each unto yourselves as you did in the beginning. I solemnly assure you that God lives and will answer your humble pleas, for he has said, "Ye shall ask whatsoever you will in the name of Jesus and it shall be done" (D&C 50:29).

19

PROTECTING OURSELVES
AND OUR FAMILIES

Latter-day Saints and other thoughtful people in many areas and nations of the world today are concerned about the growing pressures and influence of a disturbing cultural movement that downgrades social and religious values and standards of morality.

Michael Hirsely, a writer for the Chicago *Tribune*, observed that predicting America's religious future is risky business—that "the nation's most widely accepted prejudice is anti-Christian" (reprinted in the *Billings (Montana) Gazette,* 16 May 1992).

The actual signs of the times are threatening. Where will they lead? I, for one, am concerned. Previous periods of moral decline brought forth divine attention. In past times, as at present, prophets of God have delivered a voice of warning. The Lord said to Ezekiel, "I have made thee a watchman unto the house of Israel: therefore hear the word . . . and give them warning from me" (Ezekiel 3:17).

From what we are witnessing in the world around us, I am impressed to raise a voice of warning for mankind to prepare, by repentance, for the great day of the Lord (D&C 1:11–12).

I am indebted to Elder Dallin Oaks of the Quorum of the Twelve for an account—I refer to it as the parable of the bushy-tailed squirrel, the tree, and the dog—which illustrates my concern:

As two men walked across an eastern university campus, they were attracted by a crowd of people surrounding a large maple tree. They approached and noticed that the crowd was being amused by the antics of a fox-tailed squirrel circling the tree, climbing it, and running back down again. An Irish setter crouched nearby, intently watching the squirrel. Each time the squirrel ran up the tree out of sight, the dog would slowly creep toward the tree. The squirrel paid little attention as the dog crept closer and closer, patiently biding its time.

People watching this entertaining drama unfold knew what could happen, but they did nothing until in a flash the dog, catching the squirrel unaware, had it in the grip of his sharp teeth.

The people then rushed forward in horror, forcing the dog's mouth open to rescue the squirrel. It was too late. The squirrel was dead. Anyone could have warned the squirrel or held back the dog. But they had been momentarily amused and watched silently while evil slowly crept up on good. When they rushed to the defense, it was too late.

We see around us daily that which is portrayed in this parable. We sit idly by, watching as an insidious stream of profanity, vulgarity, demeaning behavior, a mocking of righteous ideals and principles invades our homes and lives through most types of media, teaching our children negative values and moral corruption. We then become upset when our children perform differently than we would wish, and social behavior continues to deteriorate.

One newspaper headline reads, "The Battle Lines Are Clearly Drawn for America's . . . Cultural War." The article then asks: "Who determines 'the norms by which we live . . . and govern ourselves[?]' Who decides what is right and wrong, moral and immoral, beautiful and ugly . . . ? Whose beliefs shall form the basis of law? . . .

"Our [cultural challenge] . . . is about 'who we are' and 'what we believe'" (Patrick J. Buchanan, *Salt Lake Tribune*, 13 Sept. 1992, A15).

A *Los Angeles Times* columnist wrote that some see "the state as either equal or superior to God in human affairs. Theirs is an uninvolved god who trickles down blessings when we want them, but whose commands are to be ignored when he asks us to do something we don't want to do.

"The fact is that our laws came from a standard of righteousness that was thought to promote the common good, or 'general welfare.' . . . That standard has been abandoned as biblical illiteracy has flourished, thanks in part to the state's antipathy toward immutable and eternal truths.

"William Penn warned, 'If we are not governed by God, then we will be ruled by tyrants.' One's view of God and his requirements for our personal lives determines one's view of the role of the state in public life. . . .

"Benjamin Franklin . . . observed that if a sparrow cannot fall to the ground without God's knowledge, can an empire rise without his aid?

"The late philosopher-theologian Francis Schaeffer wrote that 'God has ordained the state as a *delegated* authority; it is not autonomous. The state is to be an agent of justice, to restrain evil by punishing the wrongdoer, and to protect the good in society. When it does the reverse, *it has no proper authority.* It is then a usurped authority and as such it becomes lawless and is tyranny.' . . .

"This is what the culture war is about. It is conflict between those who recognize an . . . existing God who has spoken about the order of the universe, the purpose of the state and the plan for individual lives and those who think those instructions are unclear, or open to interpretation, or that God is irrelevant to the debate or doesn't exist and we are on our own. . . .

"[Thirty years ago] students could still pray and read the Bible in school, abortion was illegal and 'gay rights' meant the right to be happy. . . . The issue now is whether we will become our own god" (Cal Thomas, reprinted in *Salt Lake Tribune,* 18 Sept. 1992, A18; emphasis in original).

No wonder Isaiah, speaking under inspiration, declared, "Neither are your ways my ways, saith the Lord" (Isaiah 55:8).

Unchangeable, God-centered principles and ideals adopted by our Founding Fathers not only form the basis of freedom but are the rivets that hold it together. There is a vast difference between principles that are unchangeable and preferences where there is a choice.

There should be no question about our standards, our beliefs—about who we are!

Eyewitness accounts of participants declare the faith and courage of the converts who left their homes, as well as their families and material possessions in America or Scotland or Sweden to join with Brigham Young and thousands of pioneers in establishing the "Zion" Joseph spoke about in the Far West. Joseph Smith—their prophet, teacher, and friend—had seen God! He saw the living Christ! Few of all persons ever created have ever glimpsed such a vision: Peter, James and John, Moses, Abraham, and Adam—only a few, ever. Joseph Smith belonged to an elite group who had been tried, trusted, and found true. He was one of those described by Abraham as one of the "noble and great ones" (Abraham 3:22) who became one of the Lord's choice servants while here on earth.

Courageous and faithful people by the tens of thousands heard and believed the glorious message of a new hope for a better way of life. Did they expect to find riches at the end of the newly found rainbow? A life of comfort and ease? To the contrary! There was to be heartache, cold, pain, and hunger—with insults and injury, including tragic loss of life. It was the assurance they knew and felt of divine direction that expanded their faith to withstand such hardship.

Men and women of strong physical and spiritual strength conquered the wilderness and established what Isaiah saw and wrote of seven hundred years before the birth of Christ when he wrote. "And it shall come to pass in the last days, that the . . . Lord's house shall be established in the top of the mountains, and shall be exalted above the hills; and all nations shall flow unto it. And many people shall go and say, Come ye, and let us go up to the mountain of the Lord, to the house of the God of Jacob; and he will teach us of his ways, and we will walk in his paths: for out of Zion shall go forth the law, and the word of the Lord from Jerusalem" (Isaiah 2:2–3).

What was their purpose? What was their motive? Not for the gold in California, but that they might worship God Almighty according to the dictates of their conscience. Such was their motive—to establish the Lord's Church and teach the eternal principles revealed to their prophet,

Joseph Smith. They had risked everything they had and were willing to endure any hardship. The recorded history of their journey and of the early beginnings in the Salt Lake Valley is one of civilization's finest hours.

There was little that was inviting in this endeavor except faith. In fact, they had been warned that nothing would grow. But they were builders—not destroyers. They had a majestic dream of great things and lofty ideals: of homes and gardens, temples and meetinghouses, schools and universities. It would take work—hard work—and everyone's best efforts to make it happen. They became experienced colonizers and benefactors to our nation and to humanity. Many of us are a product of that early, inspired colonization—its teachings and blessings of the value of hard work coupled with desire and faith for a better way of life.

The depth of their faith in a living God and their loyalty and obedience, as well as their solid foundation of righteousness, inspire us today. They believed that they had started on their way toward perfection, a process to be pursued laboriously throughout a lifetime. President Kimball declared, "[But] to each person is given a pattern—obedience through suffering, and perfection through obedience" (*The Teachings of Spencer W. Kimball*, ed. Edward L. Kimball [Salt Lake City: Bookcraft, 1982], 168).

Their pathway was straight, uncluttered, unbending: they were to live the commandments of God and endure to the end. Today we know how we should live. We know right from wrong.

We are to teach and train our children in the ways of the Lord. Children should not be left to their own devices in learning character and family values. They should not be watching unsupervised music videos or television or movies as a means of gaining knowledge and understanding about to how to live their lives.

The Lord has clearly commanded that parents are to teach their children to do good, to teach them "the doctrine of repentance, faith in Christ the Son of the living God, and of baptism and the gift of the Holy Ghost by the laying on of the hands, when eight years old, [or] the sin [shall] be upon the heads of the parents" (D&C 68:25).

"And they shall also teach their children to pray, and to walk uprightly before the Lord" (D&C 68:28).

"And ye will not suffer your children that they go hungry, or naked; neither will ye suffer that they transgress the laws of God. . . . But ye will teach them to walk in the ways of truth and soberness; ye will teach them to love one another and to serve one another" (Mosiah 4:14–15).

A concerned God, by his own finger, wrote the Ten Commandments on tablets of stone. They represent the basic law of the Almighty and have formed the underlying elements of civil and religious law ever since.

The Sermon on the Mount, given by our Lord himself, details principles and instructions of heavenly origin.

Both of these divine statements of instruction—principles of which are so effectively taught in much greater detail in the Book of Mormon and the Bible and our other scriptures—if obeyed, will strengthen mothers and fathers and sons and daughters, who all have equal duty to study the scriptures and gain strength and understanding of eternal things.

The only sure way to protect ourselves and our families from the onslaught of the teachings of the world is to commit to live the commandments of God, to attend our Church meetings where we can learn and be strengthened in our testimonies and partake of the sacrament to renew our covenants, and to prepare ourselves to enter the temple worthily, where we may find a refuge from the world and a place of renewal of our capacity to cope with the evils of the world.

20

SPIRITUAL CREVASSES

One summer Clarence Neslen Jr. took his family to Jasper National Park in Alberta, Canada. They enjoyed exploring the Columbia Icefields, jumping over crevasses in the famous Athabasca Glacier. It was an exciting experience until eleven-year-old Cannon, attempting to jump across a crevasse, missed and fell into the deep chasm. He became wedged between the walls of ice. When his father looked down some thirty feet to where his son was trapped, he was further alarmed to see a river of icy water flowing beneath the crevasse.

Several young men were also exploring the glacier. They heard the cries for help and came running. They had a small rope but soon realized that it was not strong enough to pull Cannon to safety. If it broke, Cannon would most assuredly fall into the rushing river of freezing water.

Sister Neslen and others ran to a nearby lodge for help. The nearest park ranger camp was seventy-five miles away. They learned by telephone that two park rangers were near the icefields. Located by radio, they rushed to the rescue. Time was short, decisions urgent, and silent prayers were sent heavenward.

Brother Neslen tried to calm his son and soothe his fears. Hypothermia was setting in. Young Cannon's shirt had been pushed up as he fell. His bare skin was now pressed against the cold walls of the glacier. To keep his son from unconsciousness, the father called down to him to keep praying, to wiggle his fingers and toes, and to sing his favorite songs. Over and over Cannon sang:

> I am a child of God,
> And he has sent me here,
> Has given me an earthly home
> With parents kind and dear.
>
> (*Hymns*, no. 301)

All were strengthened by Cannon's faith and determination. But he was beginning to weaken. His father kept assuring him that help would soon arrive and that his Heavenly Father would hear his prayers.

The two rangers arrived. Spikes were driven into the ice, and ropes were attached to one of the rangers, who was lowered to rescue Cannon. But the crevasse was too narrow. Their only chance to rescue Cannon was to lower a looped rope and pray that he was alert enough to grasp it and then have the strength to hold on as they tried to pull him out.

Brother Neslen reported that he offered the most fervent prayer of his life, pleading with the Lord to save his son's life. "A feeling of assurance and calm came over me," he said, "and I knew that he would be saved."

Cannon had lapsed into unconsciousness. His father called down encouragement, rousing his son sufficiently that Cannon's icy fingers now were able to catch hold of the rope. "Hold on with all your might!" his father called down to him. Cannon was carefully pulled up—inch by inch, foot by foot—all thirty feet. When he was finally pulled to safety, he was unconscious. His fingers had miraculously frozen around the rope and had to be pried loose.

He was immediately wrapped in blankets and rushed to a waiting ambulance, but there was not enough warmth to raise his body temperature sufficiently. A paramedic undressed Cannon, then took off his own coat and shirt and held Cannon against his bare chest so that his body heat would radiate to the boy. Cannon slowly responded to the loving care of his rescuers. The prayers of all had been answered.

Young Cannon Neslen later told his father that, while wedged in the ice, he felt a comforting assurance that he would be saved. He knows God loves him and that He has a special mission for him to perform in this life.

Not unlike Cannon Neslen, who accidentally fell into a crevasse, some of our young people today have slipped into spiritual crevasses.

Spiritual crevasses symbolize the temptations and pitfalls that too many of our youth are tragically encountering: alcohol, with its wine coolers and keg parties; drug tampering and dependency; R- and X-rated films and videos, which often culminate in sexual immorality. On the edge of those ominous crevasses are parents and others who, with fervent prayers, cry for help and assistance. Like Cannon's father, they too pray that their sons or daughters will hold onto the extended lifeline. Their love, the teachings of the scriptures, and the assurance of the eternal blessings of the Savior's atonement are sure lifelines to safety.

Young people are not the only ones who slip into crevasses.

A stake president recently told me that a respected member who had held Church leadership positions was enticed by some business friends to try the cocaine drug "crack." The men were depressed. Their company was failing, and they succumbed to the evil enticement of illegal drugs.

The Church member wasted eighteen thousand dollars buying "crack," lost his job, underwent a personality change, and finally was hospitalized. Through it all, his wife stayed by him. She found a job, and they began the struggle of putting his life back together. His Church friends helped him get another job. His mind is seriously affected, however, and he is still somewhat dependent on some drugs. The hopes and prayers of his family are that he will be able to hold onto the lifeline.

When Satan was cast down to earth with his innumerable hosts, he became "the father of all lies, to deceive and to blind men, and to lead them captive" if they would not listen to the Lord's voice (Moses 4:4).

One of Satan's methods is to distract and entice us so that we will take our eyes off the dangerous crevasses. He has succeeded to such an extent that many no longer recognize sin as sin. Movies, television, and magazines have glorified sin into what they think is an acceptable lifestyle and there is no punishment for evil behavior. Assuredly we live in a time spoken of by Isaiah when men "call evil good, and good evil" (Isaiah 5:20).

Don't trifle with evil. You will lose. Don't display the somewhat arrogant attitude of those who say, "I can handle it," or "Everyone else does it."

A friend, visiting relatives in another state for a high school graduation, noticed a few students chewing tobacco. When he asked his nephew about it, the young man replied, "Everybody does it." My friend's nephew did not chew tobacco, but he did believe most boys did. Even in schools where in reality only a few students are using drugs, drinking alcohol, or smoking, non-users commonly believe that most of their fellow students are doing it.

Everyone is *not* doing it. Young people are influenced by their friends. Latter-day Saints are the Lord's special resource for teaching the gospel to all his other children. We are different from others who have neither our understanding nor our responsibilities. We can help set the standard.

The Lord has blessed us with special privileges and responsibilities. We were foreordained to come to earth at a time when the fulness of the gospel is on the earth. We were foreordained to receive his priesthood. The Prophet Joseph Smith said, "Every man who has a calling to minister to the inhabitants of the world was ordained to that very purpose in the Grand Council of heaven before the world was" (*Teachings of the Prophet Joseph Smith,* sel. Joseph Fielding Smith [Salt Lake City: Deseret Book, 1938], 365).

We are the Lord's spirit children, singled out with a special calling. And we know that he loves us. We have the gift of the Holy Ghost. We can discern good from evil. And with the power of the priesthood, we have the authority to represent our Heavenly Father.

To help each of us avoid the pitfalls and crevasses in life, the Lord has provided the lifeline of the precious truths in the scriptures, which, if held onto, will allow us to escape both physical and spiritual danger. The Word of Wisdom was given so that we might have clear minds and healthy bodies; the Sermon on the Mount, to make us sensitive to one another's needs; and the Ten Commandments—cut in stone by the finger of God—forbidding us to sin. He declared, "Thou shalt not."

I urge each Latter-day Saint to develop a personal companionship with the scriptures.

President Spencer W. Kimball read the Bible when he was fourteen years old—all sixty-six books and 1,519 pages. "If I could do it by coal-oil light," he said, "you can do it by electric light" (*The Teachings of Spencer W. Kimball,* ed. Edward L. Kimball [Salt Lake City: Bookcraft, 1982], 131).

President Kimball was a very special teacher for all of us. He didn't have a car or a bicycle, but he did have nine cows to milk every morning and night. He said, "I thought, 'What a waste of time, to sit on a three-legged stool. Maybe there is something else I could do while I am milking.'" He placed a copy of the Articles of Faith on the ground beside him and went through them, over and over, until he had memorized them. Then he repeated the Ten Commandments over and over until he learned them. He memorized important scriptures that would help him on his mission—all while he milked the cows. He didn't have time to waste; he had things to do with his life (*Teachings of Spencer W. Kimball,* 131).

It would be a wonderful thing for us all to use our time wisely by learning of God's ways.

President Ezra Taft Benson challenged each of us to read the Book of Mormon—the most correct of any book on earth and the keystone of our religion. As the angel Moroni sealed up the gold plates, he was inspired to promise future generations—that is, us—that on certain conditions God will manifest the truth of those records by the power of the Holy Ghost, and promising us that "by the power of the Holy Ghost [we] may know the truth of all things" (Moroni 10:5).

Imagine such a promise. If we desire with a sincere heart, with faith in Christ, we can understand all things.

Elder Jeffrey R. Holland, while working on his Ph.D. at a prominent eastern American university, got to know well one of the reference librarians who had helped him with some research.

One day he said, "Ilene, I need to know how many books we have in the University Library that claim to have been delivered by an angel."

As you can imagine, the librarian gave him a peculiar look and said, "I don't know of any books that have been delivered by angels. Swords, maybe, or chariots, but I don't know of any books."

"Well, just run a check for me, would you? It may take a little doing, but I really would like to know."

The librarian dutifully did some checking of the nine million books in the library. For several days she had nothing to report, but then one day she smilingly said, "Mr. Holland, I have a book for you. I found one book which, it is claimed, was delivered by an angel," and she held up a paperback copy of the Book of Mormon. "I'm told you can get them for a dollar. My goodness," she continued, "an angel's book for a dollar! You would think angels would charge more, but then again," she said, "where would they spend it?" (Patricia Holland, president's welcome assembly, Brigham Young University, 9 Sept. 1986).

Think of it—one book has been delivered by an angel, and it teaches of our eternal salvation. And each of us may own a true copy!

May the Lord bless us with our life's opportunities. May we put our trust in him to avoid the crevasses of sin and evil, and hold onto the lifeline of the gospel. We can make correct choices—the ones we know in our hearts will be for our best good.

21

INTO HIS
MARVELOUS LIGHT

Brigham Young University student wrote to the editor of the daily newspaper: "Why must we always tag along behind the rest of the world, trying to get as close as our religion will let us? 'A style of our own' is not an empty phrase."

Today's young people live in a world far different from that experienced by their parents. Though the world is becoming more wicked, the youth of Christ's Church can become more righteous if they understand who they are, understand the blessings available, and understand the promises God has made to those who are righteous, who believe, and who endure. All of our youth are entitled to and need this knowledge in order to combat the forces of deception that would lead them captive into darkness.

Peter, writing from Rome to the scattered Saints, understood their trials and temptations to desert the faith and go back to their old ways. He encouraged them as he wrote about "the trial of your faith, . . . much more precious than of gold that perisheth" (1 Peter 1:7). He added a broader dimension with stirring words to help us understand who we are: "But ye are a chosen generation, a royal priesthood, an holy nation, a peculiar people," and as a chosen and peculiar people, "ye should shew forth the praises of him who hath called you out of darkness into his marvellous light" (1 Peter 2:9).

While attending a stake conference, I had the blessing of meeting with a group of young people, several of whom were the only Latter-day Saints in their high schools. When I asked, "You set the right example for the rest of the students, don't you?" they replied, "We really try." As they spoke, I could see the light of belief and conviction in their faces. I could begin to understand what Peter meant by being called "out of darkness into his marvellous light."

Our youths, with all of their distractions, must realize that through their membership in the Lord's Church, they are very special, and that the Lord is counting on them so that the prophecies might be fulfilled. They are of a noble birthright and are thus different from their friends who are not members of the Church. They are a "chosen generation"; they live "in the world" but do not follow worldly trends or habits that are contrary to their belief.

Paul, writing to his beloved Timothy and realizing the pressure Timothy was experiencing, said: "God hath not given us the spirit of fear; but of power, and of love, and of a sound mind" (2 Timothy 1:7).

If our young people conduct themselves properly and develop their personalities and lives along Church standards, their candle will be high on a hill and will burn brightly for all to see.

Debbi Brown, the only Latter-day Saint in her high school senior class in Virginia, said, "It is essential for us to live the standards of the Church. Most people who know anything about the Church know that it maintains the highest moral standards. There is never a need to apologize. We are so lucky to have the true gospel. By making the Church standards *our* standards, we can share this gospel with others."

She continues: "A good friend (not a member of the Church) invited me to a party celebrating our victorious football season. He was a popular football player. I was hesitant. He knew I was a Mormon. My hesitation must have been evident. He quickly added, 'No drinking allowed.' People know our standards and respect us for them. To be different from the crowd is a privilege."

Some young people may feel at times that the Lord's commandments restrict their freedom as compared with that of others. Freedom does not mean license, nor does it imply the absence of all restrictions and disciplines. The Savior did not teach undisciplined, permissive-type freedom. When he said, "Know the truth, and the truth shall make you free" (John 8:32), he was telling us that his truth, if followed, would free us from falsity and deception; that his gospel, if followed, would free us to gain eternal life. As the light of the gospel fills our souls, our abilities increase.

One young military chaplain, a former missionary, lives the gospel as he should. His superior officer at his first duty assignment was so impressed with his spirit that he wrote: "I want you to know how much we chaplains and the thousands of men have appreciated his presence. To describe him like a breath of fresh, clean air would be poetic and not intended to demean other chaplains who labor at our large base. He has a special charisma that radiates love." The officer then added, "We have benefited in many ways from this young chaplain. We not only admire him but renew our own enthusiasm. Thousands have derived great spiritual and social benefit from his service."

Some time ago a high school senior and student body leader was asked about his relationship with his peer group. He said, "I find great strength in the example of my peers. To get up and walk out of an offensive movie, to stand up and defend or even befriend a person whom everyone else ridicules, to be the only one in the crowd to say no to drinking, dishonesty, breaking the Sabbath day—all of these actions take a person of strong character. Such people among my friends have given immeasurable courage to me and to others."

He continued, "I remember a night when some friends and I sneaked into a movie through the exit without paying. We were laughing and feeling smart and smug about it when, without a word, one of my friends got up and left the theater. Suddenly, being dishonest didn't seem funny any more. One by one each of us walked out, each secretly wishing we had had that much courage."

This young man went on to say, "Probably the most respected person I know is a young man who makes friends with all kinds of people, regardless of their belief or status. He is loved among Church members and classmates. He is always the life of the party, yet he has never lowered his high standards in any way to win a friend or to get a laugh. He gravitates naturally toward positions of leadership because his peers, even the weakest ones, sense his strength of character. He has changed the lives of many young people."

One of the great powers in the world is that of example. People need models to see and at times to lean on. Henry David Thoreau wrote: "If you would convince a man that he does wrong, do right. Men will believe what they see."

Such an example was Mervin Sharp Bennion, who became one of the renowned heroes of World War II. He was born in the small village of Vernon, near Tooele, Utah. There he grew up in a faithful Latter-day Saint home and was taught by his parents the principles of faith, reverence, respect and regard for others, confidence in himself, a strong sense of right and wrong, and an understanding of the full measure of his purpose in life. Because of his excellent reading ability as a result of studying the Bible as a small boy, he became an outstanding student in the one-room log schoolhouse in Vernon. There were usually thirty or more pupils in all grades from the first to the eighth, all taught by one teacher. The students had little time for individual instruction, but they were taught the attributes of a good character and wholesome habits, and they developed their personalities with plays and programs in which everyone participated.

Near the close of his high school days, Mervin Bennion took a competitive examination and was admitted to the United States Naval Academy at Annapolis, Maryland. There he continued his character and personality development, resulting in his being number one in his class for the first three years; in his fourth year, he dropped back to third in his class because he was tutoring as free service some of the other midshipmen who were having difficulties. When he graduated from the academy, he received the sword awarded for excellence by the Daughters of the American Revolution.

Mervin Bennion continued through the usual duty assignments of a young naval officer, growing in stature and ability and always living close to the Lord. He married Louise Clark, the eldest daughter of President J. Reuben Clark Jr., and they had one child, Mervin Jr. In Mervin's various naval assignments, he commanded a number of ships and served as chief of the Bureau of Ordnance in Washington, D. C., a distinguished position.

Wherever he was on assignment, he was always active in the Church, seeking out nearby branches and wards and attending all of his meetings. In Washington he was a counselor in the branch presidency and later served in the first bishopric of the Chevy Chase Ward. Though he was heavily involved at the Navy headquarters, he was completely devoted to his Church callings. For example, he had thirty home teaching families to visit, and he made it a point to visit each one every month. Everyone who came in contact with Mervin Bennion in the Church or in the Navy felt of his great spirit and devotion, because he knew so well his purpose in life and his responsibility.

His last assignment was as commanding officer of one of the Navy's largest battleships stationed in Hawaii, the *USS West Virginia*. America was then at peace. Commanding officers of large ships usually had free time for social life and personal affairs; however, Captain Bennion, because of his dedication and love of his country and his desire to serve well and faithfully, was careful with the use of his time. On 6 December 1941, a Saturday, he was invited to dinner at the Honolulu home of Ralph Woolley, who was serving as president of the Oahu Stake. After a pleasant evening, President and Sister Woolley suggested that Captain Bennion stay overnight and go to Sunday School with them the next morning. But he said that his place was on his ship.

The following morning, Sunday, 7 December 1941, at a few minutes before eight o'clock, Captain Bennion was in his cabin, preparing to go to Sunday School and fast meeting in Honolulu, when a sailor on watch from the bridge dashed in to report the approach of Japanese planes. Captain Bennion instantly gave the command, "Air attack! To your battle stations!" Then he ran to his own station, the conning tower on the flag bridge.

Within a few minutes the enemy planes flew in close and let go torpedoes and bombs that struck the *West Virginia* in rapid succession. Captain Bennion, anxious to see what had happened to his ship, stepped out the door of the conning tower. He had scarcely taken two steps when he was hit by a splinter from a bomb; the splinter tore into his body, and a fragment hit his spine and left hip. He fell to the floor. A pharmacist's mate rushed over and quickly bandaged his abdomen, but it was clear to him—and undoubtedly to Captain Bennion—that the wound was beyond any hope of mending, though the captain did not say a word to indicate that he knew of this serious condition.

Captain Bennion refused to be attended further and sent the man below to help other wounded sailors. As men and officers came to him, he briefly asked what was happening and gave orders and instructions. He remained courageous and cheerful and resisted, with a firmness and vigor that astonished his officers, all efforts to remove him from the bridge. He talked only of the ship and the men, how the fight was going, what guns were out of action, how to get them in operation again, who was wounded, what care the wounded were receiving, and how to evacuate them from the ship.

At about nine-thirty fire broke out, cutting off the escape of Captain Bennion and two others. The officers tied him onto a ladder and tried unsuccessfully to lift him out; then, with great difficulty and with the ship on fire, they carried him up to a navigation bridge to a corner that seemed to be free from smoke. They made him as comfortable as they could, but Captain Bennion told them to leave him and to save themselves, if possible.

From the battleship alongside the *West Virginia,* most of Captain Bennion's men watched the lone figure lying on the navigation bridge. A young ensign, deeply attached to him, watched for hours. He said that twice in the first half-hour after Captain Bennion was left alone, he saw him stir, rise up on his elbows, look about, and then drop back. The grandeur of this heroic death scene as it unfolded profoundly moved the men of the stricken fleet, and the executive officer of the ship wrote, "Mrs. Bennion, be assured that every person on the *USS West Virginia* shares your grief. We are all proud to have served under Captain Bennion, and his kindness, cheerfulness, and courage will always be remembered by all of us who had the privilege and pleasure of being under his command." Thus closed a glorious life and a naval career without fault or blemish. The following morning, when the superstructure of the stricken ship had cooled off, Captain Bennion's body was removed. The spot where he lay had been untouched by fire.

President Franklin D. Roosevelt posthumously awarded Captain Bennion the Congressional Medal of Honor. A camp at the Farragut Naval Station in northern Idaho was named Camp Bennion. And on 4 July 1943, a destroyer launched at the Boston Navy Yard was christened the *USS Bennion* by Louise Clark Bennion. Admiral David Sellars wrote to Sister Bennion, "His complete forgetfulness of self and devotion to duty at the last has set an example and will serve as an inspiration in years to come to the officers and men of the United States Navy." His heroic conduct is now cited in naval training classes as one of the outstanding examples to be found in all United States naval history.

"The most important of all his characteristics was his constant and sincere desire to keep the commandments of God," wrote his bishop. "He did not think himself overly righteous, but his sincerity and his ever-present desire to live in accordance with God's law and to perform the full duty required of him impressed all who knew him."

Mervin Bennion's character, his purpose, his desire, his faith, and his conduct were steadfastly the same. Of course, he had grown in stature and in influence, but inherently he was unchanged. He was started out on the right path by his parents in a little Mormon town, and he kept going straight ahead, his purpose clearly identified.

Each of us has been given a lamp to carry. Our lamps will light the way for us and, we hope, for others, but they must have oil. This oil will not come from the good works or the righteousness of our family or friends, but from our faithfulness in keeping the commandments of God, our actions and desires, and, of course, our love of the Master.

In Thornton Wilder's play *Our Town*, a young woman dies and discovers that she has the opportunity to live one day of her life over again. She chooses her twelfth birthday. When the day begins, her first reaction is an intense desire to savor every moment. "I can't look at everything hard enough," she says. Then to her sorrow she sees that the members of her family are not experiencing life with any of the intensity she felt. In desperation, she says to her mother (who cannot, of course, hear her), "Let's just sit and look at one another." And later she says, "Oh, earth, you're too wonderful for anybody to realize you. Do any human beings ever realize life while they live it?"

I testify that each of us, as followers of the Savior and members of his Church, can realize life while we live it, through service to our fellowman, devotion to our families, and adherence to the commandments of God. Shortly before he died, Sir Winston Churchill was invited to stand before the student body of a prestigious preparatory school in England. This was all that he had to say: "Never forsake the things that you know to be true. Never, never, never, never." May that blessing be ours.

22

OVERCOMING THE
POWER OF EVIL

A s I view the struggles of mankind in this challenging time, I reflect on the familiar verse of Henry Van Dyke that most high school students were required at one time to memorize. Van Dyke wrote:

> Four things a man must learn to do,
> If he would make a record true:
> To think without confusion clearly,
> To love his fellowmen sincerely,
> To act from honest motives purely,
> To trust in God and heaven securely.

"To trust in God and heaven securely." Wouldn't there be a feeling of great security if every Latter-day Saint home produced sons and daughters who trust in God securely and who believe in him and in his Son, Jesus Christ, the Savior of the world!

It can be difficult to think clearly in these times, to hold to a high degree of integrity and loyalty, and to maintain lofty ideals in a generation that seems to have lost its scale of values. The current wave of permissiveness in many areas of our lives is being encouraged by false interpretations of true, basic, moral principles.

The Savior warned us of these times: "There shall arise false Christs, and false prophets, and shall shew great signs and wonders; insomuch that, if it were possible, they shall deceive the very elect" (Matthew 24:24).

Unfortunately, along with much of the world, some of our loved ones are influenced by false prophets, false Christs, and modern movements of spiritualism. Some have become victims of Satanic influences because they do not understand or realize the power of the adversary, who knows human weaknesses and is ever present.

Who is this evil power? Is he real? Does he exist?

John the Revelator encapsulated that powerful struggle in heaven, the outcome of which has such an impact on all of humanity: "There was war in heaven: Michael and his angels fought against the dragon; and the dragon fought and his angels, and prevailed not. . . . And the great dragon was cast out, that old serpent, called the Devil, and Satan, which deceiveth the whole world: he was cast out into the earth, and his angels were cast out with him. And I heard a loud voice saying in heaven, Now is come salvation, . . . for the accuser of our brethren is cast down. . . . Woe to the inhabiters of the earth . . . for the devil is come down unto you, having great wrath, because he knoweth that he hath but a short time" (Revelation 12:7–10, 12).

There is an eternal struggle with evil forces. John the Revelator is speaking to all of us, telling us to be on guard, to beware.

The Lord has also warned us in modern revelation: "Wherefore, because that Satan rebelled against me, and sought to destroy the agency of man, which I, the Lord God, had given him, and also, that I should give unto him mine own power; by the power of mine Only Begotten, I caused that he should be cast down; and he became Satan, yea, even the devil, the father of all lies, to deceive and to blind men, and to lead them captive at his will, even as many as would not hearken unto my voice" (Moses 4:3–4).

In recent years, America and most other nations of the free world have been converted into a space-age Sodom and Gomorrah, aided by some publishers and movie producers, and even some so-called educators.

Moral principles have been eclipsed by the blind, ungodly pursuit of pleasure at any price.

In the Book of Mormon, Alma records Korihor's sad experience with Satan: "Behold, the devil hath deceived me; for he appeared unto me in the form of an angel. . . . And he said unto me: There is no God; yea and he taught me that which I should say. And I have taught his words; and I taught them . . . even until I had much success, insomuch that I verily believed that they were true; and for this cause I withstood the truth, even until I have brought this great curse upon me" (Alma 30:53).

Many people who believe at least tentatively in the reality of God have a much harder time believing in the reality of the devil. Some even soft-pedal the subject and go along with the popular idea that the devil is a purely mythological creature. Some roar with laughter as a television comic remarks, "The devil made me do it." Well, maybe he did! He will always try.

To deny the existence of Satan and the reality of his evil power and influence is as foolish as to ignore the existence of electricity. We know that electricity is real; we see and feel its power. We also know about war, hatred, backbiting, bearing false witness, cheating, and the broken hearts and broken homes caused by the moral sins of modern Babylon. Do members of the Church feel a lack of evidence in the reality of Satan and his power?

We are told that "some of the very elect" will be enticed and deceived, even though through baptism they have already accepted Christ as their Savior. Wouldn't the evil one concentrate on them if he found a weakness or opportunity?

A college student who hoped to repent of some serious mistakes and straighten out his life told me of an influence that, for a time, controlled his life. When he was in high school, he desired to have some expert ski equipment, so he accepted a job that would require work on Sundays and evenings. This resulted in his nonattendance at priesthood and other Sunday meetings, and he was always too tired to attend early-morning seminary. With his fancy new ski equipment, he was named to the high school ski team and made some new friends. To be "with it," he started to smoke and soon moved to marijuana and from marijuana to LSD. His parents now seemed old-fashioned, so he moved from their home in order to live with his newfound friends in an old house. His father tried to visit him and to communicate through letters, but the young man now felt completely disenchanted with Church and home. It was only after he had made many tragic mistakes that he finally came to his senses and moved back home with his parents. He told me, "The devil seemed to be in charge of my life."

After interviewing the young people in his ward, one dedicated bishop commented on the lack of spiritual direction from some parents to their own teenage sons and daughters. "Bishops and teachers can't do it all," he said. "Parents must teach their children of the pitfalls of evil." He then compared the difference in priorities in the various homes as reflected in his interviews with the youth. One girl told him, "I know the gospel is true. I keep the commandments and have no problems." Another young woman remarked, "I don't accept all of it; I'm battling with some parts. We never discuss the gospel at home."

What a tragedy! Parents must strengthen their homes and teach their loved ones to distinguish between Satan and our Savior. They must teach their loved ones that "all things which are good cometh of God; and that which is evil cometh of the devil; for the devil is an enemy unto God, . . . and inviteth and enticeth to sin, and to do that which is evil continually" (Moroni 7:12).

Taking time to explain these eternal truths of the gospel in the warm atmosphere of the home could mean the difference between exaltation and darkness. At a crucial moment, the humble testimony of mother and father recalled by a youth could make the difference in a critical decision.

True happiness in this life and in the life to come is found in keeping the commandments of God. We have been told, "You shall live by every word that proceedeth forth from the mouth of God" (D&C 84:44).

I bear witness that the devil is real. I have felt of his influence. The apostle Paul knew firsthand of his power. As Saul of Tarsus, he persecuted the Saints, locked them in prison, and spoke against them when they were put to death. Later, as the believer and great apostle, he encouraged the followers of Christ at Ephesus: "Put on the whole armour of God, that ye may be able to stand against the wiles of the devil. For we wrestle not against flesh and blood, but against principalities, against powers, against the rulers of the darkness of this world" (Ephesians 6:11–12).

If we will keep and live the commandments of God and follow the counsel of his living prophet to strengthen our homes, the protecting armor of God to which Paul refers will fit comfortably, the shield of righteousness will be sufficient for us to withstand the evil darts, and our loved ones will find great joy and salvation.

23

ETHICS AND HONESTY

James Peter Fugal was an honest man. He herded sheep much of his life in the rolling hills of Idaho—both his own sheep and those of others. One bitterly cold winter night he was herding sheep for another man when a blizzard set in. The sheep bunched together, as sheep do, in the corner of a fenced area, and many died. Many other sheep on surrounding ranches also died that night because of the weather. Though the deaths of the sheep were no fault of his, James Fugal felt responsible and spent the next several years working and saving to repay the owner for his lost sheep.

This was the type of deep moral honor and accountability that was fostered by scripture-reading, God-fearing settlers on the early frontier.

This same desire to live Christian principles was evident in Aurelia Spencer Rogers, who was schooled on the plains and founded the Primary organization of the Church. She had a concern for the moral character and social development of children. Leaders of the Primary since Aurelia Rogers have proven to be worthy disciples and continue to teach wholesomeness, virtue, and love for one another, as well as to instill a desire to understand and live by traditional values.

Some time ago Sister Haight and I attended a ward sacrament meeting some distance from our home. After the sacrament we found, to our delight, that the Primary would present the program, the theme being "We Believe in Being Honest."

I marveled at the eagerness and interest of these young children as they spoke about the fundamental principles they were learning in Primary: telling the truth, respecting the property of others, being trustworthy, and standing for the right. I thought of James Fugal, the humble sheepherder, and how wonderful it was that these children were being taught the same values that made him a man of such noble character.

As we enjoyed the Primary presentation, which emphasized timeless moral and spiritual values, my thoughts seemed to concentrate on the similarity of two important, heavenly directed events that we, as members of the Church of Jesus Christ, have special reason to be grateful for: the framing of the Constitution of the United States of America and the restoration of the gospel of Jesus Christ—each, in a significant way, sustaining the other. In addition to heavenly direction, both would require a membership of honest, virtuous people if their divine purposes were to be realized.

We attribute the rise of the American nation and its survival to two vital factors. First, God aided the efforts of those who established the republic. James Madison, who is considered the father of the Constitution, wrote, "It is impossible for the man of pious reflection not to perceive in [the Constitution] a finger of that Almighty hand which has been so frequently and signally extended to our relief in the [establishing of our republic]" (*The Federalist*, no. 37 [New York City: Modern Library, n.d.], 231).

Second, America's citizens were known for their righteous conduct and example. This is best expressed by Alexander Hamilton, a soldier turned statesman, who wrote that "it seems to have been reserved to the people of this country, by their conduct and example, to decide the important question, whether societies of men are really capable or not of establishing good government from reflection and choice, or whether they are forever destined to depend for their political constitutions on accident and force" (*The Federalist*, no. 1, 3).

The important human attributes needed for this new nation to really

160

become a cooperating and workable republic of separate states would be manifested by a people who demonstrated by their lives a belief and desire to live in a society of justice for all mankind. Likewise, the Lord, through the Prophet Joseph Smith, recognized that, like the new nation, the restored gospel would have difficulty enduring without men and women of similar integrity and conduct.

On 1 March 1842, Joseph Smith, at the request of Mr. John Wentworth, editor of a Chicago newspaper, composed thirteen brief statements known as the Articles of Faith, which summarize some of the basic doctrines of the Church. As the concluding statement, the Prophet wrote this inspired code of conduct:

"We believe in being honest, true, chaste, benevolent, virtuous, and in doing good to all men; indeed, we may say that we follow the admonition of Paul—We believe all things, we hope all things, we have endured many things, and hope to be able to endure all things. If there is anything virtuous, lovely, or of good report or praiseworthy, we seek after these things" (Article of Faith 13).

What an inspiring description of good people, God-fearing people, people committed to deal justly with mankind! These would be the type of people who could raise up a nation and help it survive, and the kind of people to comprehend the true gospel of Jesus Christ with the needed faith to proclaim it to the inhabitants of the earth.

People throughout the nation and the free world, are indebted to freedom-loving individuals everywhere who had the faith and integrity necessary to build the foundations of our societies upon fundamental moral values. Only in an atmosphere of freedom and trust could values like honesty and integrity truly flourish and thus encourage others to pursue their rights to liberty and the pursuit of happiness.

Therefore, it is with great alarm that we read newspaper accounts and hear daily media reports that describe the decline of moral decency and the erosion of basic ethical conduct. They detail the corrupting influence of dishonesty, from small-time, childish stealing or cheating to major embezzlement, fraud, and misappropriation of money or goods.

Headlines and feature stories dramatically demonstrate the need for honesty and integrity in family relationships, in business affairs, and in the conduct of government officials and religious ministries. Recent stories in major national publications emphasize the need for public concern over the direction in which we are moving.

Public virtue, which expects men to rise above self-interest and to act in the public interest with wisdom and courage, was so evident in leaders like George Washington, who, we used to declare, could never tell a lie, and Abraham Lincoln, known as "Honest Abe." In the past few years we have seen "official after official—both on the national and the local political scene—put self-interest . . . above the larger public interest. . . . Men and women have . . . been removed from federal office and even gone to jail in our times because they exceeded the limits set by the framers of our Constitution [and God's commandments]" (Charles A. Perry, "Religious Assumptions Undergird the Entire U.S. Constitution," *Deseret News,* 27 Sept. 1987, A-19).

One reason for the decline in moral values is that the world has invented a new, constantly changing, and undependable standard of moral conduct referred to as "situational ethics." Now individuals define good and evil as being adjustable according to each situation; this is in direct contrast to the proclaimed God-given absolute standard: "Thou shalt not!"—as in "Thou shalt not steal" (Exodus 20:15).

A recent Gallup Poll indicates that the vast majority of Americans want schools to do two things: teach our children to speak, think, write, and count; and help them develop standards of right and wrong to guide them through life. However, some teachers avoid questions of right and wrong or remain neutral or guide children into developing their own values, which is leaving many children morally adrift.

Many of our youths have either lost the knowledge of what is right and what is wrong or were never taught these basic values. President Harold B. Lee's classic statement that "the most important of the Lord's work that you will ever do will be the work you do within the walls of your own home" is most certainly true today. "Ours is the responsibility as parents to teach our children chastity . . . [and not only to be morally clean but to be] faithful [and] valiant, striving to live [all of] the Lord's commandments" (*Strengthening the Home* [Salt Lake City: The Church of Jesus Christ of Latter-day Saints, 1973], 4, 7–8).

Some adults, including public officials and civic leaders, have also been led astray by longings for luxury and leisure.

The devastation that comes to the families and loved ones of those convicted of crimes such as stealing, fraud, misrepresentation, child abuse, sexual transgression, or other serious crimes is immeasurable. So many sorrows, heartaches, and even broken homes result from a false belief that people can set their own rules and do what they want to do as long as they don't get caught.

Individuals may deceive and even go undetected or unpunished, but they will not escape the judgments of a just God. No one can disobey the word of God and not suffer for so doing. No sin, however secret, can escape retribution and the judgment that follows such transgression. We declare: "There is only one cure for the evils of this world, . . . and that is faith in the Lord Jesus Christ, and . . . obedience to [His] commandments" (Mark E. Petersen, *Improvement Era*, Dec. 1963, 1110).

We run the risk of losing both our domestic freedom and eternal salvation if we circumvent by greed and avarice the ethical and moral strictures inherent in the Constitution of this land and in the gospel of Jesus Christ. The continued survival of a free and open society is dependent upon a high degree of divinely inspired values and moral conduct, as stated by the Founding Fathers. People must have trust in their institutions and in their leaders. A great need today is for leadership that exemplifies truth, honesty, and decency in both public and private life.

Honesty is not only the best policy, it is the only policy!

Someone said, "We have committed the Golden Rule to memory. May we now commit it to life." The Savior's teaching, "Therefore all things whatsoever ye would that men should do to you, do ye even so to them" (Matthew 7:12) should be the basis for all human relationships.

The Lord is very clear about the conduct he expects from the inhabitants of this earth. Nephi declared: "And again, the Lord God hath commanded that men should not murder; that they should not lie; that they should not steal; that they should not take the name of the Lord their God in vain; that they should not envy; that they should not have malice; that they should not contend one with another; that they should not commit whoredoms; and that they should do none of these things; for whoso doeth them shall perish. For none of these iniquities come of the Lord; for he doeth that which is good among the children of men; . . . and he inviteth them all to come unto him and partake of his goodness" (2 Nephi 26:32–33).

The time is now to rededicate our lives to eternal ideals and values, to make those changes that we may need to make in our own lives and conduct to conform to the Savior's teachings. From the beginning to the end of his ministry, Jesus asked his followers to adopt new, higher standards in contrast to their former ways. As believers, they were to live by a spiritual and moral code that would separate them not only from the rest of the world but even from some of their traditions. He asks nothing less of those who follow him today.

Do we really believe in being honest, true, chaste, benevolent, and virtuous? On this test may hinge the survival of our society, our constitutional government, and our eternal salvation.

24

THE FIGHT AGAINST PORNOGRAPHY

I n recent years a plague of pornography has swept across most countries of the world with increasing momentum and devastating impact. What began a few years ago as a few crude picture magazines that startled sensitive people has grown to hundreds of publications, each seeking to outdo the others with increasingly shocking content.

So-called adult bookstores, selling materials that appeal to the prurient mind, are now open in nearly every city. Obscene materials once available only by mail and in a plain brown wrapper are now prominently displayed on the magazine racks of many local convenience stores and other business establishments where they are readily accessible to the young and the old alike. Theaters showing R- and X-rated films and worse have become established in most cities. It is reported that one particularly offensive movie, filmed at a cost of forty thousand dollars, has earned revenues of many millions of dollars.

It should come as no surprise that grand juries have found that 90 percent of all pornography is dominated by organized crime. Large profits from one project become a source of funds for still larger and more sophisticated enterprises as a growing tidal wave of smut dashes against the weakening bulwarks of morality.

New technologies that can bless our lives in many positive ways are being used also to spread pornographic corruption. Video recorders and computers can bring to homes great classics of music, history, art, and drama; but they can also bring into some of these same homes lurid portrayals of debauchery that contaminate those who view them and extend their corrupting influence to our communities and society.

Cable television and satellite transmissions, with their powerful capacity for good, are not only being used, but are also being abused. State and national laws necessary to govern their proper use are not yet established, and they are almost totally unregulated. Greedy men have been ready to exploit this vacuum in legal regulation without regard for the consequence to its victims.

Some may ask, What is pornography? United States Supreme Court Justice Potter Stewart said that while he could not exactly define pornography, "I know it when I see it" (*Jacobellis v. Ohio,* 378-U.S. 184, 1964).

Pornography is not a victimless crime. Who are its victims? First, those who intentionally, or sometimes involuntarily, are exposed to it. Pornography is addictive. What may begin as a curious exploration can become a controlling habit. Studies show that those who allow themselves to become drawn to pornography soon begin to crave even coarser content. Continued exposure desensitizes the spirit and can erode the conscience of the unwary. A victim becomes a slave to carnal thoughts and actions. As the thought is father to the deed, so exposure can lead to acting out what is nurtured in the mind.

But there are other victims. Crimes of violence have increased in the United States at up to five times the rate of population growth. A 1983 University of New Hampshire study found that states having the highest readership of pornographic magazines also have the highest number of reported rapes. Pornography degrades and exploits men, women, and children in a most ugly and corrupt fashion.

Perhaps the greatest tragedy of all is in the lives of children who become its victims. The saddest trend of our day is the alarming increase in child abuse. Much of it occurs within families and involves corrupting the divine innocence that children have from birth. The Savior reserved his harshest condemnation for those who offend little children. He said: "Take heed that ye despise not one of these little ones; for . . . it is not the will of your Father which is in heaven, that one of these little ones should perish" (Matthew 18:10, 14).

The Lord commanded: "Neither commit adultery . . . nor do anything like unto it" (D&C 59:6). President Spencer W. Kimball declared: "The early apostles and prophets [warned against] sins that are reprehensible . . . —adultery . . . infidelity . . . impurity, inordinate affection . . . sexual relations outside of marriage . . . sex perversion . . . preoccupation with sex in one's thoughts. . . . And one of the worst of these [sins] is incest . . . [or] sexual [relations] between persons so closely related that they are forbidden by law to marry" (*President Kimball Speaks Out* [Salt Lake City: Deseret Book, 1981], 6). Incest is an ugly sin, and this particular sin may damage its innocent victims well nigh irreparably.

What impels offenders to such terrible deeds? Police report that some 80 percent of those who molest young boys and girls admit modeling their attacks on pornography they have viewed. How has this evil gained such a foothold in our society? Have we ignored the warnings of our Church leaders? President Kimball declared: "So long as men are corrupt and revel in sewer filth, entertainers will sell them what they want. Laws may be passed, arrests may be made, lawyers may argue, courts may sentence . . . men of corrupt minds, but pornography and . . . insults to decency will never cease until men have cleansed their minds. When . . . [man] is sick and tired of being drowned in filth, he will not pay for that filth and its source will dry up. . . . Hence it is obvious that to remain clean and worthy, one must stay positively and conclusively away from the devil's territory, avoiding the least approach toward evil. Satan leaves his fingerprints" (*The Miracle of Forgiveness* [Salt Lake City: Bookcraft, 1969], 229, 232).

This growing presence of obscenity has been aided by the lowering of media standards for advertising, by relaxed movie ratings, by soap operas and situation comedies on television that use their powerful voices to justify, glamorize, and encourage sexual relations outside of marriage.

Perhaps we have been intimidated by those who claim that

producing, distributing, and using obscene materials is a basic right to be defended. This is not true. Even under the divinely inspired constitutional principles of this land, obscenity is not condoned nor protected. The United States Supreme Court has clearly held that criminal prosecution of those who produce and distribute obscene materials does not violate their First Amendment rights (*Miller v. California,* 413 US 15 [1973]).

This spreading evil has been aided by a failure to enforce laws designed to prohibit or regulate it. Although some additional legislation may be helpful, those who have been fighting the discouraging battle against pornography in recent years are in agreement that nearly 90 percent of all obscene materials could be eliminated from our communities if existing obscenity laws were strictly enforced. A few courageous cities have performed outstanding service by ridding themselves of X-rated theaters and so-called adult bookstores and by limiting access to hard-core pornographic books and magazines. The citizens of Mt. Lebanon, Pennsylvania, formed a citizen action group and determined that they were not going to allow such degrading material in their community. They closed an adult bookshop and a large distribution warehouse, and, as a result of their determined citizens' organization and involvement, they have had enacted a city public-nuisance ordinance.

Lawmaking bodies will listen to effectively organized citizens. However, too often the trend is tragically toward citizen apathy and a sense of futility. And who is to blame? We could conveniently point the accusing finger at public prosecutors who are not vigorously enforcing the law; we need men and women of courage and conviction in these offices of public trust, if the awful tide is to be stemmed. But while one accusing finger is pointing toward those who make or enforce the law, another may point to us who may be equally to blame.

Fortunately, what is deemed legally obscene is partially determined by local community standards. We as citizens, by our own standards, are the ones who can help establish what offensive materials are—which ones are legally obscene—and cannot claim protection from the law. Unfortunately, many people assume that even hard-core pornography is legal because it is so prevalent. But that is not true. Some public prosecutors may excuse themselves from seeking enforcement of obscenity laws by explaining that community standards determine what is obscene. They therefore conclude that because the community tolerates such material, its presence must reflect the accepted community standard. Concerned citizens—you and I—can change this misunderstanding.

What, then, is needed to reverse this ominous insult to us, to our families, and to our communities? Only when men and women concerned for their families and communities let their voices and their influence be felt in thoughtful, rational ways will we alter the destructive course on which we are traveling. Silent indignation may be misinterpreted as approval. Irrational action may be ineffective because it is regarded as prudish rather than thoughtful. Albert Camus wrote: "By your actions or your silence, you, too, enter the fray."

May I suggest a few things we could do to halt this deadly evil:

1. Let all of us resolve to keep our minds, our bodies, and our spirits free from the corrupting influence of everything that is obscene and indecent. Let it have no place in our homes, our minds, or our hearts. The psalmist David wrote, "Who shall ascend into the hill of the Lord? or who shall stand in his holy place? He that hath clean hands, and a pure heart" (Psalms 24:3–4). If you have in your possession offensive materials that should be destroyed, let this be the day of decision and action. If you have been tempted or have even considered abusing or offending a child, confess and repent and forsake such evil thoughts or actions.

James, the apostle and the brother of our Lord, wrote: "Blessed is the man that endureth temptation. . . . Let no man say when he is tempted, I am tempted of God: for God cannot be tempted with evil, neither tempteth he any man" (James 1:12–13).

Let us discuss with our children of appropriate age, and in sensitive ways, the harmful effects and addictive nature of such material. Let us rigidly monitor the selection of television programs, movies, videocassettes, music, and other forms of entertainment for our families. Let us foster in our homes a love of knowledge through uplifting literature, wholesome books, carefully selected movies and television programs, classical and exemplary popular music, entertainment that uplifts and edifies the spirit and mind.

2. Let our voices be heard in our communities. If something offends our standards of decency, we should speak up. Let us persevere in our efforts to work with local groups to establish a visible relationship with other like-minded citizens and seek to preserve our quality of life by encouraging steps against such material.

If appropriate, let us approach the management of offending stores, movie theaters, bookstores, television and radio stations, with a request to withdraw indecent materials from public display or use or patronage. Of course, such efforts should be consistent with the constitutional process, exercising gentle persuasion.

Some nationally owned and franchised convenience stores and others have responded to the courteous request of their customers to discontinue selling certain degrading materials. We commend them for what they have done and would encourage others to follow their lead.

3. Let us make our own elected officials and law enforcement people aware that we support the enforcement of laws prohibiting obscenity and regulating indecency, thank them for their past service and present efforts, and encourage them to continue the difficult and sometimes thankless task of strictly enforcing the existing laws in a consistent and fair manner.

4. Where legislation is needed to meet new technological advances in cable and satellite transmission, let us support the enactment of reasonable laws and regulations that would help reduce the number of those whose lives will otherwise become marred by addiction, child abuse, and many of the other social ills that pornography helps foster. The laws should be carefully drawn within constitutional limitations, so that the freedoms we seek for ourselves now and in the future are not denied for others.

5. Let us exercise our faith and prayerfully seek help from God our Father in this vital task. There are some who believe that the pornography industries are out of control, already too powerful to curb. I would disagree with this dim view, but I also recognize the immensity of the task before us. We know that people of good will, united in such a worthy

cause and aided by divine power, can overcome any obstacle and meet any challenge to help our Lord and Savior to bring to pass the immortality and eternal life of man.

"There is a line of demarcation," said President George Albert Smith, "well defined, between the Lord's territory and the devil's. If you will stay on the Lord's side of the line, you will be under his influence and will have no desire to do wrong; but if you cross to the devil's side of the line one inch, you are in the tempter's power, and if he is successful, you will not be able to think or even reason properly, because you will have lost the Spirit of the Lord" (quoted in Kimball, *Miracle of Forgiveness*, 232). As a man soweth, so shall he reap.

May we strive continually to purify our personal lives, strengthen our homes, and recognize the evil forces that are working through insidious ways to thwart our eternal progress.

25

THE SACRAMENT:
A DIVINE OBLIGATION

I wish everyone could grow up in a small town. I have so many happy memories of my boyhood. During those delightful summer and winter days, we created most of our own activities and amusement. They were wonderful days.

The most important building in our town, in addition to the schoolhouse, was our ward meetinghouse. The chapel had an imposing, two-tiered, elevated stand. The first or lower tier had a table for the ward clerk at one end and a piano at the other end, and right in the center of this elevated area was the sacrament table. On the highest level of the stand were the pulpit, with a red plush cover, and beautifully carved chairs with red plush seats for the bishopric or visiting authorities. On the rear wall of the chapel were two impressive oil paintings, one of the Kirtland Temple and the other of the Salt Lake Temple. Everyone in attendance had a clear view of the stately pulpit and, of course, the sacrament table.

Sacrament meetings were very special occasions. The Lord instructed that "it is expedient that the church meet together often to partake of bread and wine in the remembrance of the Lord Jesus" (D&C 20:75). We of the Aaronic Priesthood knew it was special. We were well trained. We knew exactly what we should do. We had been taught at home and in our quorum meetings of the high honor placed on us as holders of God's holy priesthood, which authorized us to perform sacred ordinances of the gospel.

As a deacon, I vividly recall how we admired the two priests, seated up on the first level of the raised platform, who would administer the blessing on the sacrament of the Lord's Supper. Everyone in the meetinghouse could see them. I'm sure the two priests felt the importance of the occasion. They were neatly dressed in their best clothes and were well prepared. They acted and looked as dignified as members of the bishopric, who were seated in their special chairs above them.

As deacons and teachers, we sat on the first row, prepared to pass the sacrament. I recall how shiny the bread trays appeared, and how the glass cups for the water sparkled. Everything about the sacrament table, including the linen, was immaculate.

Everyone was expected to sing the special sacrament hymn. Everyone did sing. Children were trained not only to be reverent but also to know some of the words of the most familiar sacrament songs. I can still see Sister Ella Jack, who led the music, standing in full view between the sacrament table and piano. Before the hymn started, she would pause and look over the congregation to be sure everyone had a hymnbook and was ready to sing. She gave special attention to see that the Aaronic Priesthood boys had hymnals. We would all sing.

We were learning in our youth that in order to feel of the Spirit, we must experience a change in our hearts, and in order to be in harmony on this sacred occasion, we had to sing the sacrament hymn. As we sang the words, our souls were better prepared to understand this sacred ordinance. At the Last Supper the early apostles joined with the Savior in singing. Matthew records, "And when they had sung an hymn, they went out into the mount of Olives" (Matthew 26:30). As we young boys would sing in sacrament meeting, the message of the words would be impressed upon our hearts. There comes to one's soul heavenly thoughts as he joins in heavenly expressions coupled with heavenly melody.

After the sacrament song had been sung, the priests knelt on a little red velvet bench and offered the blessings on the bread and the water. We didn't have printed cards, but the Doctrine and Covenants was open to section 20, if needed. There were no microphones or speakers. The priests were taught to read slowly and distinctly and to enunciate clearly so that everyone might hear and understand the words of these sacred prayers, every word of which was given to us by the Savior himself.

Our quorum advisers schooled us in priesthood meeting on the sacredness of the ordinance of the sacrament: about how our thoughts should be of the Savior, about his sacrifice for us, about the importance of our dress and appearance, and about this quiet opportunity to resolve in our own minds to do better in keeping all of the commandments.

We would watch carefully as the priests officiated in a sacred procedure somewhat similar to the very first such occasion, and listen as they recited the divinely directed blessings upon the bread and water in remembrance of the flesh and blood of our Savior. Every word in the sacrament ordinance is vital. All who attend the sacrament meeting should clearly hear each word and reflect upon the covenant being made and on their own personal worthiness.

The ordinance of the Lord's Supper was introduced by the Savior himself, as recorded by the Gospel writers. Elder James E. Talmage wrote:

"While Jesus with the Twelve still sat at table, He took a loaf or cake of bread, and having reverently given thanks and by blessing sanctified it, He gave a portion to each of the apostles, saying: 'Take, eat; this is my body.' . . . Then, taking a cup of wine, He gave thanks and blessed it, and gave it unto them with the command: 'Drink ye all of it; for this is my blood of the new testament, which is shed for many for the remission of sins.' . . . In this simple but impressive manner was instituted the ordinance, since known as the Sacrament of the Lord's Supper. The bread and wine, duly consecrated by prayer, become emblems of the Lord's body and blood, to be eaten and drunk reverently, and in remembrance of Him" (*Jesus the Christ* [Salt Lake City: Deseret Book, 1983], 553–54).

This holy ordinance was later taught by the Savior to the Nephites in the Western Hemisphere. After teaching and healing their sick, "Jesus commanded his disciples that they should bring forth some bread and wine unto him. . . . He took of the bread and brake and blessed it; and he gave unto the disciples and commanded that they should eat. And when they had eaten . . . , he commanded that they should give unto the multitude."

He instructed, "Give it unto the people of my church, unto all those who shall believe and be baptized in my name. And this shall ye always observe to do, even as I have done, even as I have broken bread and blessed it and given it unto you. . . . And this shall ye always do to those who repent and are baptized in my name; and ye shall do it in remembrance of my blood, which I have shed for you, that ye may witness unto the Father that ye do always remember me. And if ye do always remember me ye shall have my Spirit to be with you. And I give unto you a commandment that ye shall do these things. And if ye shall always do these things blessed are ye, for ye are built upon my rock" (3 Nephi 18:5–6, 11–12).

This weekly opportunity to partake of the sacrament of the Lord's Supper, one of the most sacred ordinances of The Church of Jesus Christ of Latter-day Saints, is further indication of his love for all of us. Associated with the partaking of the sacrament are principles that are fundamental to our advancement and exaltation in the kingdom of God and the shaping of our spiritual character. We should reflect in our own weekday conduct the spiritual renewal and the commitments made on Sunday.

We all have regrets for words or deeds or thoughts from Sabbath to Sabbath that we would like to erase from our souls. Perhaps we have erred against or injured someone. If there are ill feelings in our hearts, we should repent, obtain forgiveness from those affected or transgressed against, and then humbly, with contrite spirits, prepare ourselves to be worthy to partake of the sacrament. If we sincerely repent, we can be forgiven and spiritual healing can come to our souls.

By revelation, the Lord instructed that "the members shall manifest before the church, and also before the elders, by a godly walk and conversation, that they are worthy . . . —walking in holiness before the Lord" (D&C 20:69). He also taught: "Ye shall not suffer any one knowingly to partake of my flesh and blood unworthily" (3 Nephi 18:28). Some years ago Elder Melvin J. Ballard wrote: "I am a witness that there is a spirit attending the administration of the sacrament that warms the soul from head to foot; you feel the wounds of the spirit being healed, and the load being lifted. Comfort and happiness come to the soul that is worthy and truly desirous of partaking of this spiritual food" (*Crusader for Righteousness* [Salt Lake City: Bookcraft, 1966], 133).

During the administration and passing of the sacrament, those present have the opportunity to think of the precious gifts available through the Savior's sacrifice for each of us, for the sacrament is blessed and sanctified so that each may partake of it in remembrance of him (D&C 20:77). We have the opportunity to reflect on his life; to recall with deep gratitude and reverence his example of purity, kindness, and love; to reflect upon his great atoning sacrifice; and to partake of the symbols of his torn flesh and his blood that was shed on the cross. He taught the Nephites, "I came into the world to do the will of my Father, because my Father sent me. And my Father sent me that I might be lifted up upon the cross; . . . that I might draw all men unto me" (3 Nephi 27:13–14).

As we partake of the sacrament and reflect upon his sacrifice for each of us, we make a solemn commitment to keep the commandments he has given us; by so doing, we might always have his spirit to be with us. By partaking of the sacrament each Sunday, we receive the encouragement and strength to keep the commandments of God, to live uprightly, virtuously, and honestly. He himself summed those commandments up as follows: "Love the Lord thy God with all thy heart, and with all thy soul, and with all thy strength, and with all thy mind; and thy neighbour as thyself" (Luke 10:27).

This is what every person who partakes of the sacrament is committed to do. Living God's commandments obligates each of us to a life of goodness and to exclude from our lives hatred, enmity, immorality, selfishness, drunkenness, jealousy, and dishonesty.

May we experience the joy of regular attendance at sacrament meeting and feel the blessings of eternal progression in our personal lives through wholehearted compliance, in spirit and actions, with the sacred words of the sacrament. The Prophet Joseph Smith taught: "Reading the experience of others, . . . can never give us a comprehensive view of our condition and true relation to God. Knowledge of these things can only be obtained by experience through the ordinances of God set forth for that purpose. Could you gaze into heaven five minutes, you would know more than you would by reading all that ever was written on the subject" (*Teachings of the Prophet Joseph Smith,* sel. Joseph Fielding Smith [Salt Lake City: Deseret Book, 1938], 324).

The sacrament is one ordinance that allows us to experience a personal relationship with God and enlarges our knowledge and understanding of him and his Only Begotten Son.

Our personal reward for compliance with the covenants and obligations in the ordinance of the sacrament is companionship of God's Holy Spirit. This is the light that leads to eternal life. The divine virtues associated with the partaking of the Lord's Supper are (1) keeping his divine life ever in mind; (2) loving him with all our heart, might, mind, and strength; and (3) laboring to bring to pass his ultimate purpose—the eternal life of man.

26

Seek Ye First the Kingdom of God

I am thankful for good music and for the influence of good music in our lives. When we sing "For the Strength of the Hills" (*Hymns* [Salt Lake City: The Church of Jesus Christ of Latter-day Saints, 1985], no. 35), I think of the strength that I have felt throughout my life—the strength that we receive by being faithful, obedient members of the Church. Living as we should becomes our strength of character.

My grandfather had been living in Farmington, Utah, for a few years before he and his family were asked to go out into south-central Idaho and help settle a new community to be named Oakley. My father, Hector, was a teenager when they moved. My mother, Clara, was a teenager living in Tooele, Utah, when her father was asked to move to Oakley and build the first flour mill there. And so Hector and Clara fell in love out in that little Idaho town.

When it was time to be married in 1890, they didn't ask where they would be married and what they would do. They knew what to do. Oakley is about 180 miles from the Logan Temple, but my parents went to the Logan Temple from that little town to be married on 15 May 1890. I've often wondered how they made the trip. Imagine one of the old double-seat surrey buggies without any sides on it, pulled by a team of horses.

I don't know how many were in the company, but if you would imagine a modern automobile—with its steel top, glass sides, heaters, radio, comfortable seats—by the side of that buggy, you would see a great difference. Imagine those young people with some of their party organizing to travel 180 miles. It would take a week. They set out to make the seven-day trip to the temple in that buggy. They were without sleeping bags or winter clothing as we know it today, but they had clothing that was appropriate for that time, some blankets and quilts, and some flour sacks filled with food.

So when we sing about the strength of the hills, we should thank the Lord for the strength of where we are and who we are and what we believe in and how we live. Are the young people today wondering if it would be inconvenient for them to go a few miles to the Manti Temple or the St. George Temple or the Atlanta Georgia Temple or even to the Stockholm Sweden Temple or the Johannesburg South Africa Temple or wherever it might be? Picture in your mind what went on only a few years ago, and your travel to a temple will not seem so inconvenient.

My wife, Ruby, and I were married in the Salt Lake Temple on 4 September 1930. The next morning we went to see her mother on M Street in Salt Lake City to bid her good-bye. And as part of those tender moments, she fixed a little basket of food for us to put in the car. She said to me, "David, promise me that you'll take good care of Ruby." And I said, "I promise." I remind Ruby periodically that someday I'm going to see her mother again, and I hope I will be able to look her straight in the eye and say, "I think maybe I've done it."

Ruby and I were married the right way, sealed in the temple with its divine covenants and commitments that promote trustworthiness, faithfulness, devotion and dedication. Now, after more than sixty-five wonderful years, we look back on our time together and realize that it gets better as time goes on.

When Ruby and I left for California in 1930 in our little Model T Ford, we crossed Nevada going a hundred miles an hour on those gravel, washboard roads—thirty miles straight ahead and seventy miles up and down. We'd never been to California before, so when we finally made it to Lake Tahoe, that large lake looked warm and beautiful. I didn't know that it was icy cold under the first inch of water. We found a little motel and went in and put on our swimsuits. I wanted to demonstrate to her that she had married a real "he-man." We went on the pier out in the lake, and I thought it looked so wonderful. The sun was just going down. I dived straight down, to demonstrate to Ruby what a "find " she had made. As I dived through the icy water farther down, I thought I was a goner. I clamored to get out.

We had a wonderful time together as we drove on to Berkeley, California. We found a furnished apartment for forty-five dollars a month. But our second day, when I came home that evening, I discovered that my key wouldn't work in the door. I finally went to the manager and said, "I'm sorry, my key doesn't work." She said, "Oh, that's all right. Your wife has moved you." I said, "Moved us?" "Yes," she said, "we had another apartment that was five dollars less per month."

Ruby and I figured out one day that we have moved around the United States twenty-seven times. We moved to California on three different occasions. We moved to Illinois twice. We've moved back and forth and around. But out of that, we look back upon it all with joy. Now, with our three children and our fifty-plus grandchildren and great-grandchildren, we say, "What a wonderful life has been ours."

If we seek first the kingdom of God and live as we should, all the rest of life seems to fall into place and wonderful things happen. So as we look upon our family, we are pleased that all who could of our grandsons and some of our granddaughters have served missions. They all understand and can sing "I Am a Child of God" (*Hymns,* no. 301) and other wonderful songs of Zion. We're proud of them. Life is rich and full and wonderful. It all falls into place if we help it by the way we live.

As we reflect upon the sesquicentennial year of our pioneers' arrival, we remember their trek across the plains—the suffering and the living in the wagon beds and sleeping out on the ground and walking barefooted and burying the dead out on the prairie—finally to arrive in the valley of the Great Salt Lake, there to establish Zion. You can imagine how they would later sing, "Let the mountains shout for joy! / Let the valleys sing" (Evan Stephens, "Let the Mountains Shout for Joy," *The Choirbook* [Salt Lake City: The Church of Jesus Christ of Latter-day Saints, 1995], 50).

We can do that now as we reflect upon our ancestors who were part of that trek and all that they have done in making the way for us and then envision the Church today. As we reflect upon what is happening throughout the world regarding the image of the Church, the growth, and the continued expansion of stakes and wards and membership worldwide into new countries, new areas, again we could sing with great enthusiasm, "Let the mountains shout for joy." Here we are, and the word is spreading the way it has been predicted and the way it should be done.

I'm getting old enough now that I just about span the twentieth century. Not long ago President Hinckley was talking about a dedication coming up in the year 2000. He said to me, "And I'm planning on your being there." I said, "I'll plan on being there." If I can make that date, I will be ninety-four years old, for I was born in 1906. That would give me 94 percent of the one hundred years of this century.

As I reflect upon the twentieth century and what I have learned, I would like to say something about what I have witnessed and what I have felt during that time.

In the year 1906 the population of the Church was about 360,000 people. There were fifty-five stakes. There were twenty-two missions. There were some fifteen hundred missionaries, as far as I've been able to calculate, which would mean about seventy missionaries per mission in twenty-two missions. The work was moving forward the year that I came into existence.

The story was told by my mother that on the morning I was born, on a Sunday, my father was quite proud. He was the bishop of the Oakley First Ward in Oakley, Idaho, and he went outside to announce it to one of our Scandinavian friends, Brother Petersen, who was walking by. My father asked him to come in and seen the new son. My mother said I was the homeliest little child she had ever seen. I was undernourished, wrinkled, and bald headed. And so Brother Petersen, after looking at me, said,

"Sister Haight, do you tink he's worth boddering with?" Well, that was my entrance into the world.

And now from that time I've seen automobiles come into being, and the first airplanes. I've seen radio develop from a little crystal with a "cat whisker" to tune it, to the beginning of the modern electronics world. I remember that we would sit in the Idaho Power Company at night with a little radio and scratch with that little whisker, and we could get some terrible static. We thought we were tuned in to China because we couldn't understand what was going on.

As I think of the world that I knew when I was young, the basic values that we talk about were in place then. With all of the things that I've seen happen while I've lived upon the earth, nothing has come along to change those values. We now have the great ability to communicate as rapidly as we do and in the various ways that we do. We can travel faster—through the air, in automobiles, and so on—but the basics, the eternal principles, haven't changed a bit.

I was ordained a deacon by Bishop Adams, who took the place of my father when he died. My father baptized me, but he wasn't there when I received the Aaronic Priesthood. I remember the thrill I had when I became a deacon and held the priesthood, because I had been taught in a simple way that I had received the power to help in the moving forward of the Lord's program upon the earth. We receive that as twelve-year-old boys. We go through the ranks of the lesser priesthood—deacon, teacher, and then priest—learning little by little, here a little and there a little, growing in knowledge and wisdom. That little testimony that we start out with begins to grow, and we see it magnifying and building in a way that is understandable to us. We can feel the magnitude of it as we start to grow up and prepare for manhood.

Speaking of preparing for manhood, I was a man by the time I was twelve because my mother expected it of me. She was not looked upon as a widow; she was my mother, with the responsibility to rear, to teach, and to train us and to help us prepare for life. And so I would say, remember the simple, simple basics that we learn from the beginning, that we're taught in the scriptures.

Starting with Adam, the basics were upon the earth, and with the development of mankind, and the speed of automobiles or airplanes or communication, none of those gospel basics has changed. They're still in place. We have to learn to obey the simple, basic rules of the gospel.

The gospel is true, and it will move forward to fill every corner of the earth. People will have an opportunity to hear with their own ears that Jesus is the Christ, the Son of God. Of him I testify.

SOURCES

The messages in this book have been adapted from the following sources. The addresses were given in general conferences except as noted.

"Become a Star Thrower," *Ensign*, November 1983, 39.

"Call to Serve, A," *Ensign*, November 1988, 82.

"Challenge for Future Missionaries, A," address delivered at Brigham Young University, 17 March 1997.

"Come to the House of the Lord," *Ensign*, May 1992, 15.

"Ethics and Honesty," *Ensign*, November 1987, 13.

"Families Are Forever," *Ensign*, November 1976, 20.

"Feed My Sheep," *Ensign*, May 1979, 62.

"Filling the Whole Earth," *Ensign*, May 1990, 23.

"Jesus of Nazareth," *Ensign*, May 1994, 75.

"Joseph Smith: The Prophet," address delivered at Brigham Young University Fifteen-Stake Fireside, 2 March 1986.

"Love All," *Ensign*, November 1982, 10.

"Marriage and Divorce," *Ensign*, May 1984, 12.

"Missionary Work—Our Responsibility," *Ensign*, November 1993, 61.

"My Neighbor—My Brother!" *Ensign*, May 1987, 59.

"People to People," *Ensign*, November 1981, 54.

"Personal Morality," *Ensign*, November 1984, 70.

"Personal Temple Worship," *Ensign*, May 1993, 23.

"Planting Gospel Seeds of Spirituality," *Ensign*, January 1973, 74.

"Power of Evil," *Ensign*, July 1973, 54.

"Prophets Are Inspired," *Ensign,* November 1996, 14.

"Seek First the Kingdom of God," *Ensign,* November 1995, 73.

"Solemn Assemblies," *Ensign,* November 1994, 14.

"Spiritual Crevasses," *Ensign,* November 1986, 36.

"Successful Living of Gospel Principles," *Ensign,* November 1992, 74.

"Sustaining a New Prophet," *Ensign,* May 1995, 36.

"Temples and Work Therein," *Ensign,* November 1990, 59.

"The Basics Have Not Changed," *Ensign,* May 1997, 37.

"The Resurrected Christ," *Ensign,* May 1985, 59.

"The Sacrament," *Ensign,* May 1983, 12.

"The Sacrament—and the Sacrifice," *Ensign,* November 1989, 59.

"This Work Is True," *Ensign,* May 1996, 22.

"We Beheld His Glory," *Ensign,* May 1977, 7.

"Your Purpose and Responsibility," address delivered at Brigham Young University, 4 September 1977, 129.

INDEX